The Voyage of Cultivation

Derrick E. Sumral

abbott press®

A DIVISION OF WRITER'S DIGEST

The Voyage of Cultivation

Abbott Press books may be ordered through booksellers or by contacting:

Abbott Press
1663 Liberty Drive
Bloomington, IN 47403
www.abbottpress.com
Phone: 1-866-697-5310

ISBN: 978-1-4582-0034-1 (sc)
ISBN: 978-1-4582-0080-8 (hc)
ISBN: 978-1-4582-0033-4 (e)

Library of Congress Control Number: 2011915017

Printed in the United States of America

Abbott Press rev. date: 09/21/2011

There is only one thing that can come from the collaboration of Derrick Eugene Sumral, the man, and Poetry, the art . . .
and that is . . .

Desoetry . . . the journey . . .

Contents

Train up a child in the way he should go, and when he is old he will not depart from it. Proverbs 22:6 NKJV

Introduction

Beginning at an early age, I have always had a fascination with words. Being a fatherless child exposed me to experiencing confusion, interests, and concerns that were, at times, uncomfortable for me to openly and outwardly express. Over time, and through time, I learned to use my fascination to express myself in written form when I was uncomfortable expressing myself verbally.

The Voyage of Cultivation is a collection of poems and expositions written in direct correlation to my life. *The Voyage of Cultivation* is a documentation of my maturation as a human being, a man, a writer, and, most importantly, as a Christian.

Emotionally charged, I set sail from being a small boy with a big heart to running a gauntlet of sensitivity and sensuality lined with beautiful and unsuspecting females, from marriage to divorce to adultery to abortion, from spiritually struggling to surviving back to struggling. *The Voyage of Cultivation* shines light and splashes color on issues of life that would otherwise be dark and dull.

Underlying the conquering of heavy and controversial issues, the purpose of *The Voyage of Cultivation* is to inspire anyone who reads of its entirety to take their life, in whatever shape it is in, and reshape it into the best life that it can possibly. Transitioning from simple four-line poetry to striking symbolisms and witty wordplay, *The Voyage of Cultivation* is, itself, a symbol of taking something small and mediocre and crafting it into a great and positive tool for cultivating one's life. Journey through *The Voyage of Cultivation* and be inspired to overcome and, most importantly, grow.

BOOK I

The Preparation

CHAPTER 1

The Beginning . . .

The Mac

He sees a gorgeous girl he does not know.
From his mouth, slobber starts dribbling to the flo'.

He walks up to, he's thinking about scoring.
But when she sees him, she thinks he's boring.

He says to her "You're like a shooting star,
With those graceful legs, traveling far."

Time is passing along, just wasting away.
Then some other mac comes and steals her away.

My Moms

Short is my mother, like a Keebler's elf,
But still she found the height to put my books on the
shelf.

She says, "Go into the world and make momma proud.
Just be yourself and never try to fit in the crowd."

Her voice could be related to a six year old kid,
But could be heard loud like Stentor's did.

She studied Jeopardy; she knows the answers by heart.
She studies the Bible and now asks me "How art…?"

My Moms is a good person as you can see.
That's why she is the only person that means the world to
Me.

CHAPTER 2

Itchy Finger

What You Are

For the twinkle in your eye,
Like a shining star;
To seek your beauty
I'd travel far.

Luscious lips
And soft fingertips.
From your lovely hips,
Fleshly oil drips.

Silky, smooth skin
From face to feet.
Tasteful meat
Too sweet to eat.

Elegant personality,
Bubbly like wine.
Voluptuous voice,
Sends a chill down my spine.

During the night,
I would like to peep
Into your window
To watch your beauty sleep.

In my bag of emotions,
There's a feeling that lies;
Waiting to be revived
By a gaze from your eyes.

In my heart for you,
There is a thing called love.
Pearly white
And pure like a dove.

I'll cherish you forever
In the place called my heart.
You Gorgeous Earth Angel
That's what thou art.

What I Like

Why does everyone
Have something to say
When I talk to what I like
When it walks my way?

People tend to stare,
But I don't care,
When I talk to a girl
With long, blonde hair.

Sometimes I wish
People could understand:
I like **all** girls,
Not one brand.

Asian, Black, Indian,
Latin, or White:
I'll cuddle with either one of them
All through the night.

I like girls
Who are attractive and smart:
Someone I'd smother
With the love in my heart.

What I like about a girl
Are the qualities within.
I don't pay too much attention
To the color of her skin.

I like girls
Who are faithful and true.
Sweet, sexy, and seductive
Just like you.

If I Could

If I could,
I really would
Tell her something
Really good.

There are too many,
To count the ways
She makes me feel
Throughout the days.

I should tell her,
But I hold back.
For it is courage
That I lack.

I want to tell her
How I feel,
About this love
That is so real.

She is my joy.
She is my pride.
Why do I keep
My feelings inside?

I shouldn't have to tell her.
She should see
The feelings I show
So obviously.

She's on my mind
All day and night
I would tell her,
If I had the might.

Someday I'll tell her,
So she will know
About my river of love-
For her it flows.

The Scar

Closed the door,
Turned opposite of right.
Stranded metal steals my skin
Like a thief in the night.

Proceeded down the hall
Unaware of my condition.
Getting to the doughnut table-
That was my mission.

Perverted scruples
Where inserted in my pupils,
As a million and a half questions
Are thrown at me by school pupils.

Into the bathroom I go
To let loose my liquid waste.
On the floor there is blood
That trickled from my face.

At the sight of blood
I went to the reflecting glass,
And saw the depth of my injury In its full mass.

Being the egotistical male,
That all men can be,
Told to myself,
"This won't affect me."

Stepped into my class,
Teacher stopped my pace.
Was sent to the nurse,
So she could fix my face.

As I live my life,
Curious people will peek
At the three and a half inch scar
Left upon my cheek.

To Have You

To have you
Would be a dream come true.
So much joy
With many things to do.

I could hold you in my arms
And nibble on your lips.
Run my fingers through your hair
And caress your fingertips.

Embraced in a realm of passion
As your chest lies upon mine.
A tasteful aura arises,
As our lips become intertwined.

Fore-playful thoughts about you
Run loosely through my mind.
My hands feel like a wandering traveler
As they rub on your behind.

To keep from going too far
I keep your lips in sight.
Massaging the skin of your back
While our tongues playfully fight.

Oh, how tempting it is
To try to get inside.
But I choose abstinence
To stay pure of sex and pride.

Making sweet love to you-
That will have to wait.
Spending our life together-
That should be our fate.

To have you
Would be a dream come true.
To tell the truth, I want you,
And you probably never knew.

A relationship with you?
I think I'm ready.
For it is a great desire of mine
To have you as my steady.

What Is It?

When I wake from my sleep
My mind is on you.
My head is full of thoughts
Of things to say and do.

When I see you walk & talk
I can only watch in awe.
There is something about you
That tightly locks my jaw.

My thoughts from the morning,
They somewhat die.
I lose all train of thought,
But I don't know why.

I think of whispering in your ear
While you blush & laugh,
But my mouth gets so weary
Like a new born calf.

I try to talk,
But I feel like a bore.
All I can do is watch you
While my thoughts drop to the floor.

I'm not a nervous person
So I cannot explain
Why my emotions get aroused
By the call of your name.

There's just something about you.
It has forced me into a verbal drought.
I wish I knew what to do;
Something to help me out.

I wish I knew what it is.
It has my oral cavity so stressed.
It seems like an evil spirit,
But in a way, it's still finessed.

I'll soon conquer this thing.
Watch and you'll see.
I'll soon gather the courage
To ask you to be with me.

The Unknown

Sometimes I wonder if
You feel for me inside.
I often think you do,
But quite well, your feelings, you hide.

I've questioned my heart
To see if it is true.
But there is no question in my mind
That my feelings are only for you.

Surely you know
How I feel for you.
But I'm not sure if you feel the same for me
I wish I only knew.

Maybe you are innocent
And never was aware.
Although you may have felt like telling me,
Your inner person wouldn't dare.

Maybe you hide your feelings on purpose
To make the challenge fun.
If so, I'll keep on playing
For the game is yet to be won.

Visions of us rush through my mind,
But, in reality, it is not the same.
Reality is practically in my grasp,
But uncertainty of my unknown remains.

Sometimes the unknown can be playful,
Sort of like a tease.
Leaving me yearning for an answer
And weak & weary in the knees.

Maybe I'm worrying too much.
I may be feeling insecure.
If so, that lets me know this one thing:
My feelings for you **are** for sure.

The Kiss

I paid her a visit
And her parents were there.
Usually, that causes nervousness,
But there was none in the air.

As we were watching a movie
She lied down on the floor.
Taking a glimpse at her legs
My heartbeat began to soar.

As we laughed & talked
She unknowingly became a tease.
In effect, I began to daydream
About her lips in which I wanted to please.

Into the living room she called me.
Then we were all alone.
It was time for me to unleash
My spontaneous plan full-blown.

She challenged me to a game of cards,
But the game was already lost.
For I had not played in quite a while,
But for her I'd pay the cost.

Losing the game of cards
I jokingly began to cheat,
While lying there daydreaming
Of the chance for our lips to meet.

It's soon time for me to leave,
But I didn't want to go.
For I have waited anxiously
For us to stand mouth to mouth … toe to toe.

In the outside air, I told her I wanted her lips.
She didn't feel the same.
She said that she didn't see me in that way.
Why? Neither of us can fully explain.

The fact that I could be intimate
Was a fact she could not believe.
The thought of she & I kissing
Was one she would not conceive.

Gazing at the stars
On the pavement we stand,
As I put my thoughts to action
And interlocked the fingers of our hands.

I pulled our bodies together
Reaching the end of my conquest.
I rested my forehead upon hers
As her breast pressed against my chest.

I stared into her eyes
While revealing my desires from within.
Suddenly, our lips gently touch;
The kissing game begins.

Momentarily magnetized,
Our mouths became as one.
Gentle, sweet touching
Were the actions of our tongues.

After the kissing stopped
She said, "I won't complain."
And deep inside her heart I knew,
As before, she didn't feel the same.

After speaking ending words
We went our separate ways.
But I can't stop thinking about the kiss
That set my heart ablaze.

Even though I might've asked too much
When I asked her to be my girl,
But always in my memory will be the kiss
That made my emotions twirl.

Un: Touchable, Believable, . . . Forgotten?

Mass confusion hit me
Right from the start.
Uncertain about my feelings-
Fake or from the heart?

For a while I had no answer,
But I soon realized
Why visions of you were be-stilled
In the pupil of my eyes.

You are untouchable, unbelievable,
And never the least unforgotten.
Bushels of joy you've given me
Kept my heart warm like blankets of cotton.

Extraordinary qualities in you-
God hath given too much,
Like tender feelings & looks
Too delicate to touch.

No other girl can touch you.
You stand on a higher ground.
No choice to be under superiority,
Around your finger they're wound.

Why are you untouchable?
Here's the reason why-
You're my ever-blooming flower.
Other girls wither & die.

It's somewhat unbelievable,
The affect you have on me.
When thoughts of you enter my mind,
Nothing else seems to be.

It's hard to believe all of the splendor
God has put into one soul.
But if it weren't for that splendor
You wouldn't be my goal.

It's hard to believe that you are human.
Your elegance is so unreal.
You sometimes seem supernatural
Due to the way that you make me feel.

It's unbelievable how you keep
My heart's candle lit.
That's why you're the only girl
That I'll truly never forget.

For me to forget you is like
An orange without its peelings;
No one in remembrance for
Whom I have overwhelming feelings.

Unforgettable nights of
Staring into the skies.
Holding you in my arms,
Gazing into your eyes.

How could I forget
Those lollipop lips?
Like streams of tasty nectar
All sweetness drips.

Nor can I forget
Your perfect personality;
Sophisticated brainwaves
Stimulating excellent sensuality.

Totally unforgettable-
The reality of a dream;
That of a baby nippling,
Making your rosebuds gleam.

Holding an untitled emotion,
But it is truly the way I feel-
You are the only girl for me;
True to me, but to you it's UnReal.

Swings

Life is a repetitive parabolic motion;
Like the motion of a set of swings.
From all the pain it gives
To all the joy it brings.

From the beginning you need strength
To get the motion started,
And you take the risk of succeeding
Or falling short, becoming broken-hearted.

Let's say that you make it;
You're in the groove of things.
But you take it for granted and forget
That life is a set of swings.

You're on top of the world!
You have it all … so you think.
But soon you come swooshing down-
Back to the beginning's brink.

Your stamina pulled you through,
But you thought you were finished.
Once again you climb high;
All sorrow has diminished.

You've gotten a little higher this time.
You feel you can't be stopped.
You still feel the joy of the top,
While a form of gravity has you dropped.

Happiness lasts the majority of time.
Depression lasts a short, small while.
It could be the results your actions-
The actions of a Bible bibliophile.

Your longevity of happiness
Is a blessing not of shame.
Blessings given accordingly
To the praising of His name.

Dedicated to those pursuing excellence
In the lifestyle of Christianity

What Can I Do?

Though my words may be few,
They are from my heart and very true.
Girl, just tell me what I can do
To fulfill my dream of me and you.

Versus

That of a spider spinning webs
For catching food, generally flies,
Was the intention of my mind
When her image filled my eyes.

I tried to put her on the side
And keep her out of my mind.
But she would & could not hide
And my thoughts she did find.

At the bottom of the barrel,
She had nothing at all to lose.
My top prospects, they fell short
And she stepped up and filled their shoes.

I wanted to converge with this girl,
But it was going to be hard.
With too many girls in my mind,
I had to stop and discard.

Billions of girls,
Well, it seems, in my scenes-
Left like that of droppings
Of trees of tangerines.

All this done
For the sake of one broad.
Question is—Do I want her?
Neither nay nor a nod.

It's kind of odd,
That I don't know the solution.
The intentions of my mind,
She contaminated like pollution.

Someone new arrives.
Should've known. It never fails.
This "new girl" caught my girl
Like a pack of sitting snails.

Unknowingly,
These two girls were in versus.
Never saying a word
While their separate actions converses.

The "new girl" was for me.
This I knew, well, I thought.
But for nothing in this world
Being with me she wouldn't be caught.

The "new girl" was a mess
And I had to let her go.
Even though it was too late,
Her true feelings she did show.

In a matter of no time
The first girl re-stakes her claim.
She does it cautiously,
Like a lioness hunts her game.

Hiding underneath a front-
A wall full of resistance,
I was drowning in the affects
Of her sweet & tender persistence.

She had her plan caged away
Like the colors in a prism.
Then she quickly lets it loose
Like a blitzing cataclysm.

Like a surrendering soldier,
I gave in with no restraint.
I let this girl come into my life
And there is not one complaint.

I thought the time would never come-
When I would love one girl.
But, yet, she is the one-
She is the "queen" of my world.

Stage Fright

Butterflies of nervousness,
Rattling of the knees.
The last childhood level
Of learning ABC's.

The senior year in high school:
People say it'll quickly end.
But no matter what they say,
The fear is still within.

Academic expectations
Causes shaking in the shoes.
Trying to escape the pressure,
Stress steps in and blows a fuse.

Scared of disappointment
You're frantically running around.
Juggling the options of your life
While your priorities have you bound.

It all comes to an end.

The diploma is in your hand.

But inside, there's **still** fright,

There's still a stage on which you will stand.

CHAPTER 3

The Calm Before the Storm

Neither a Beginning,
Nor an End

¿...if love were two cliffs through which a river ran through,

would love be the bridge that connects the two?

Could love be portrayed by the embrace of blades of grass by the
morning dew?

Might love be the bond between the sea and the beach?

Or might it be the desire for that certain star that is so far out of
reach?

Could love be so strong that it turns steel into dough?

Or could love attract a queen to an ordinary Joe?

When you hurt someone's feelings and it hurts you inside,

is it love that causes tears in spite of your pride...?

¿Love?

Does love make beauty appear better than it seems?

Or does love bring you more pleasure from your reality than it does from your dreams?

Honestly, there is no true explanation of love, but at any given moment that I hear the word, you're the only person that I am thinking of.

Everlasting

I would walk a never-ending mile

To re-live the first time I saw your smile.

From the first touch to the first kiss—

You're the one. All others hit and miss.

My purpose in social-ness became defined

When our separate identities became intertwined.

Our togetherness is like the Moon and the Sun,

An everlasting relationship that can't be undone.

Four Seasons

A thin line for when used dirt is reborn
But there are evident new seeds and rains of pour.
New life begins to form, seemingly trite and true
Everything begins to start again, all seemingly new.

The sun smiles on many faces helping things grow
Frozen waters that used to trickle endlessly flow.
This seems to be a joyous time; everyone knows your name.
You can't help but to frolic around with rest of the hunted game.

"What is that? I don't know. Was it a chilled breeze?
Who the fuck dimmed the lights? Why they changing the leaves?
What the hell? Go wit the flo'. Stick this thing through.
Gather everything you need, make it suitable for you."

The preparation paid off. This world is fuckin' cold.
This is the unseen moment of truth. Spring and summer had you
sold.
Slipping on the ice, the chill aggravatingly chaps your lips.
Is this where I lose my mind and all my remaining reality slips?
Maybe you were a fool; next time stay true to **yourself**.
Uh-oh! There's spring right around the corner; smirkingly offering
health.

What, How, When, Where, Who?

What? My friend. The only one in whom I can truly trust and depend.

My lover. The only one who deserves my love whether in public or under a cover.

My mate. The joining of our souls were destined; meant to be; fate.

My wife. My pride, my joy, my everything. The centerpiece of my life.

How? Whether like a diligent aggressor or with the gentleness of a dove,

I will always and forever find a way to express my never-dying love.

The dawn can bring its beauty and the darkness of midnight can bring its wrath,

I will never waiver from completely pleasing you, no matter what the path.

When? All day and every day, my life and love are promised to never leave you.

Should it be needed and even when it is not, my love is always ready to please you.

I will always be there for you, at the tip of a hat, at the drop of a dime.

Simply stated, when it comes to my love for you, there is no such thing as time.

Where? Wherever. There is no place too big or too small to show my appreciation.

A special somewhere or a nothing nowhere; wherever you need my love: that's my destination.

My mind. Continuous thoughts of loving and pleasing you are always there.

No need for you to worry or for you to fret, me and my love aren't going anywhere.

Who? My wife, Kyronna Jan Sumral. Who else would, could, should it be?

There never was, is currently not, and will never be anyone who'll make me feel this way than she.

She is the one who completes me. She is the life within my life.

She is my gift. She is my treasure. A love from above, she is my wife.

…change is inevitable …. change is the one thing of **this** world that will always remain consistent … change is the focal point of this piece … change is the connection between the previous piece and the following … change is why this piece is not as *customary* as my previous piece … change is why the catalyst of this "connection" will not have its elaborate details depicted in a poem … these vague phrases are all it is worthy of … however, the catalyst was life-changing … for three lives … one for the better … one for the worse … and the other: it's up in the air … in contrast to the inevitable, some things remain the same … I want, desire, and need for the same things as before … my ways of obtaining them have *changed* … *evolved* is a better term … evolution is change in which the latter is better than what it was before … my thoughts, concerns, interests, needs, and desires have not changed, but evolved … and so have my ways … I will never change again … only evolve … and the same goes for her; only she is no longer her … she is now who … and who is this evolution of the woman that I want, need, and desire …

Seasoned

The uncertainty of mixed emotions will never be explained.

Why does it seem sunny today, cold tomorrow, and the day before, it rained?

Confusion is frustrating, your world says, "#@&% it, I'm done."

But change is inevitable; you can't see, but only feel the continuous sun.

The days are bright, full of love with an abundance of life.

You ask from where? Well, the nourishment of the day and the moans of the night, right?

Highs can't last too long; you'll never always have it all.

Regardless if you want it, you need it and the shades from the tree will fall.

Passion and heat has faded; yet beauty is now serene and is calling your name.

Colorful changes and sweetened silence; not too much joy, not too much pain.

Nevertheless, change is back. This time you're not ready and it seems a little too bold.

Deep breaths are hard to come by; the whirlpools of winds are way too cold.

No life. No hope. Life is hollow and seems to be at an unfathomable end.

Dejected and alone, unsure if your personal self is even a friend.

As if being in a daze, present growth has passed and your world again is confused.

Did I gain anything from the past? Was that time well used?

For the ever-changing seasons of this man, there will never be an end.

One can only wish and be so lucky to experience said times with a friend.

A friend with a mind, body, and spirit seasoned with compassion with no secrets untold;

A woman of desire, love, and commitment would have to fit the mold.

Intelligent, patient, beautiful, charismatic, sexy, tried and true;

Never will there be someone as close to that as you.

If it is to be, then it will happen … within the season of my life.

And granted, that friend should be you: a lady, lover, companion, and eventually-everlastingly my …

Friend

What a short, simple word. But it possesses great complexity. If you asked *n* amount of people what "friend" meant to them, you'd probably get *n* amount of answers. If 58 people were asked, then 58 different answers would be given. I'll even say that all of the different answers would have an extent of hyperbolized glorification. And they would probably use "friend" differently in their lives. Is "friend" overused? Generally, phrases are overused. But can a simple word like friend become cliché as well? You hear people, all of the time, saying things of the such: "That's my friend," "Is so-and-so your friend," or "a real friend wouldn't do that." The ones that really get me are "my good friend" (as if one would say another is their "bad" friend) and "my best friend". Is there such a thing as a "worst" friend? It seems that a friend, whoever they may be, has some level of expectancy placed on them. Expectations, in most cases, stem from contractual (give-and-take) agreements, whether it is verbal, written, rhetorical, and that of sensual obviousness (the 5 senses). An employer would expect an employee to do his work, since said employee is getting paid. If I told you that I would give you $5 tomorrow, then you would be expecting $5 from me sometime tomorrow. A customer ordering a #1 from McDonald's would expect a Big Mac in return, since that was the product that was advertised. A boxer would expect to get punched since he agreed to punch as well. It is funny how friends *expect* from each other as if there was a contract. There is one word that makes all of the difference. Selfishness. Everybody wants something, whether it is tangible or intangible. The question is do you just want to get what you want or are you willing to give to get what you want? And I'm talking about giving of yourself without the expectation of receiving something in return. What there should be is a *looking forward to* between friends (without give-and-take). How about looking forward to honesty. Understanding. Loyalty. Consideration. Laughter. Comfort. Here's a good one: companionship. It could be husband/wife companionship in the journey of life or just companions in laughter; sharing the same feelings about a joke. Now, I know that people are individuals, making them different in mind & thought, which could lead to conflict/friction; but restating this might help: understanding. There is always a solution. Maybe people are too impatient to notice. Too lazy, even? It's just too easy to just go and find a "new" friend real quick. Over-usage can be dangerous. Just finding a "new" brings negativity to the "old". Let's think about it. Is there negativity in what comes to your head when you think of the word "friend"? I doubt it. If there is, then why continue to use "friend"? Maybe a small word such as "friend" **can** become cliché.

CHAPTER 4

Rome Is Burning

Narcissistic

Lord you've outdone yourself. What a work of art I am!

I **will** go on and describe myself, but in one word, just say, "Damn."

There are so many great things about me; to describe, where do I begin?

It would take more than a million lifetimes to go from the beginning to the end.

Attractive is an understatement; no one's looks will ever compare.

Sitting all by myself, even the air would have to stare.

My body is so inviting; corrupting the thoughts of both bad and good.

Not a soul is deserving. To have it, one can only wish they could.

My visual appeal is just the beginning because my voice is yearned to be heard.

Makes no difference to whom I speak; their ears are kissing every word.

The simple sound of my name makes all heads turn.

Like it or not, the mentioning of me draws all concern.

Speaking of concern, all, great and small, adore my caring heart.

My compassion overflows; all would partake of it if they were smart.

The world shall never know another being as selfless as me.

I know. It's hard to fathom; however, my time is, but should not be, free.

For the effect of my sense of humor, one would go an extra mile.

At times, even in silence, my aura alone brings to all a smile.

In a nutshell, that is me. One must say I'm a tough act to follow.

With the endless irresistible things about me, everyone else must be hollow.

Diamonds and dogs are no best friends for me. Just give me myself.

No one else to give unconditional love: richer or poorer, sickness or health.

This train of thought is so narcissistic. How arrogant could I possibly be?

The truth is … when I think of me, **YOU** are all I see.

Delilah, Jezebel, Stella

A lioness after her king, you know, but not of what she *wants*.

An angry, but awe-struck "bully"; cute are her harmless taunts.

Rhetorically stealthy in confidence, her appeal, she distinguishingly flaunts.

Out of the blue, she wants you; but pshhhhhh, you don't care.

Your peace of mind? It's as if she simply strives to be a wear.

You seem to be, but not to be, experienced. Your fragrance is becoming her air.

Sharing the wealth, you are getting yours and she is definitely getting hers.

No pressure. No folding. But you give in because she is simply working your nerves.

A drink of a rainbow ... not this time. For it is the vintage wine your taste deters.

It was for you; well, for the others who wanted you. They labeled you "hung."

"You're the best at being the worst." You should've seen the double-edged tongue.

Do you see the thin line now? Her bells are rung and her birds have sung.

Delilah slithered in and dethroned you. You're a deity with no power in his finest hour.

Jezebel's misery needed company. She tore down a weakened tower.

Mmmmmm. Stella's eventual blossom brought joy like that of a biannual flower.

She's there solely for herself … and, maybe, a little for your shame.

She hurts; therefore, you shall hurt. She yearns to see your pain.

She's there because you've taken her there, riding the sound of your name.

Separately, they hail mighty. Their own worlds they do tame.

Scarily, one can become another, or the other; hence being one in the same.

Tree House

Standing at ground level and staring straight ahead,

An occasional peripheral glance reassures you're not alone.

Circling the trunk you wonder if this is really where you're to be led.

The dangling limbs and branches attract you. That *tree* you're going to own.

"Make haste. Be cautious. That branch looks to be too far away.

You can't make the wrong move. You may fall and hurt yourself.

If I don't go now, then I won't go at all. Who knows what after today?

Someone else could get there first. Then I'd never forgive myself."

Creeeaaak. Something is telling you not to stay there for too long.

Momentarily paralyzed, you stop and then quickly grab the closest limb.

With beads of sweat on your brow, you silently sing a "thank you" song.

Ironically, it was a stroke of genius but realistically done on a whim.

Taking a deep breath, you notice a rope and, to it, you dream to draw nigh.

For it seems to be the best way up and no one else will ever know.

The knotted rope is quite inviting, but you eventually release a sigh.

You need "unreal" strength to climb the rope: please avoid the woe.

You surprisingly find tree climbing to be more brain than brawn.

Yet you are very fatigued and you really desire to rest your feet.

An untraditional house you stand before. It has not a fence or a lawn.

In reminiscence of how you got there, your journey seems to be obsolete.

"No _____'s allowed?! There's no way that I'm not getting in."

An unseen voice demands a password; frustration is looming near.

You turn the knob and the door is locked. You begin to hang your chin,

Until "Wait! I have an idea," and you appealingly grin from ear to ear.

"This tree house is great. I didn't think the inside would be this cozy."

The tedious journey taken to get here was well worth the time.

"Let me re-close this window. That should keep out the nosey."

This place that seems so perfect has no room for anyone else's grime.

Surely, there is some company. The resident can't be gone.

"I'll just lie down and rest a while. Here's a nice spot on the floor.

Would it be okay to stay overnight? I'll just leave the lights on."

Gasping and startled from slumber, it sounds like that unseen voice is knocking on *your* tree house door.

Ladybug

Your presence alone brings pure fascination.
The sight of you, from loneliness, brings emancipation.

So sweet, gentle, and mild, you come my way.
Your beauty brings light to the darkest and even the brightest day.

Any chance of our paths to cross, I'm submissive to the sound.
A queen with not *true* king; no manbug to be found.

Deep inside, I want the ladybug solely to myself.
When one has but has not, should they be blessed with such a wealth?

Yes, a beauty you are, but what is it like to feel your touch?
When near or far, in a ponderance of time, one spendeth much.

Only a certain few will feel her; it is said to be luckily finessed.
But what if she knew of whom all along and through her touch she confessed?

There's no real testimony to tell of her love,

But one can only speculate that it is given from God above.

Ladybug, like a priceless ruby, well deserved is your worth.

There's no touch other than yours that is sought for more throughout all the Earth.

Internal Fire
(I Know, But I Don't Care)

There is nothing in life more precious than the ones you adore.
I truly adore our friendship, but my heart desires more.

My mind drifts away at times and I know why.
It is consumed by thoughts of you; that, I won't deny.

I don't want one like you; I simply want you.
To covet is a sin you say; well, that, I already knew.

I do know you and I are not likely to be,
But the description of my ideal woman fits you to the tee.

I know for us to be, there would have to be some dismay.
If it were to come to pass, on your every aspect, my all would lay.

Your love and life are already committed. I don't expect you to share.
But I know if there came a time when you needed me, I would be there.

My rubbing thoughts and feelings result in an internal fire.
Not a love. Not a lust. For now…just a passionate desire.

My Dear Lady,

Am I perfect? No. A gentleman? Well, you tell me. You, perfect? That's no as well. A lady? Enough for two. For our paths not to cross would be a catastrophe. A man am I wanting to meet your every need in the realm of sensuality; being selfless to you in giving my all, but selfish in being a completed man through the joy of completing you. A man's wealth does not come from any monetary source, but accumulates through gratification and satisfaction from being the sole source of pleasure of his woman.

Granted, you are strong and independent; however, the fact remains that everyone needs that someone: man for woman and vice versa. I'm that someone, that man. When your mind is cluttered because everyone except the right one is talking in your ear; I am that sweet sound of silence that is therapy for the mind. The hush that massages your thoughts and serenades your ideas. For when your eyes are tired, I am your sight for sore eyes. Ever have that favorite something where when you think of it you can just simply taste it and the flavor never seems to fade? My love is that taste and I am that favorite something. When the wind blows, I am the passing fragrance that makes your mind's mouth water and melts your heart. When your desire for stuffed animals seem child-like and your need for pillows becomes bland, you can hug and squeeze me. I am your source of warm coziness. A warmth of simultaneous taking away of aches and pain and giving of comfort and joy. When you stand proud, I will be your sturdy foundation; providing strength and support. Tired and weary? Feel like resting? I am your bed of rose petals. Your candle-lit bubble bath. Your special place of confiding solitude. Your solution before the problem.

Who is looking after me, you ask. Well, a person can't give of something without receiving it first. The things that one gives of himself or herself as a person are a small portion of what they have learned from being with, around, or watching another. I give of what I receive from you. It is said that man and woman are made to complement each other. This is my compliment: what I am to you is a mirror image of what you are to me.

I am you,

Derrick E. Sumral

BOOK II

The Journeyman

CHAPTER 5

The Ring . . . Removed

First Encounter

Bare breast and gyrating hips,
Lustful and alluring stares fill the air.
The desires of men at my fingertips,
Yet, in the midst, questioning why I'm there.

The work of these broads was not the best
I'd seen better bodies here before.
On the brink of leaving disappointed
There came a sweet voice I just could not ignore.

It was inquiring why I was sitting alone.
I said that I was waiting for **her** to sit with me.
I had brightly replied out of sheer, quick wit,
Not knowing how true that response would be.

In shorts, a t-shirt, and a du-rag,
I was shocked the waitress' focus was on me.
I had not seen her all night until then
And I gave no stare, glare, gesture, nor a plea.

Flirtatious conversation: simple, yet, sensual
And I sensed a mutual desire for something more.

I said "masseuse". She said "a massage indeed,"
She let my hands be the flirt: something I adore.

My fingers gently walked the course of her nape.
My lips yearned to caress her sweet smelling skin.
Instead, I leaned to look upon her vibrant visage:
She had her eyes closed and a seductive grin.

A lucky green clover and a secret message;
On the waist, but no waste, was a lovely dragonfly.
All of them therapeutic to the touch
And ever-so pleasing to the eye.

Hands in motion and fingers frolicking,
They could not resist the small of her back.
Lurking below were teal and lavender panties
My hands turned savage and wanted to attack.

Her giggles graciously grabbed my attention.
Now my mind was on the hunt for foreplay.
But my hand's pleasure island had work to do,
And I thought, "It surely can't end this way."

Away she went with her tray in hand.
I'd bring her back if I had control of her thighs.
And as if there was a kindred familiarity,
She looked back and we both winked our right eyes.

Starriness and solitude sat next to me again.
It seemed as if boredom had no end,
When, once again, like a Godsend
Came my luscious, back-bearing friend.

I was pleased to know she wanted my company.
Unfortunately, and truthfully, I could not partake.
But we know when and where the other would be;
A new dawn will come for us to wake.

Beautiful

Not quite a quarter-of-a-century old, I've had the opportunity to see **and** meet some very beautiful girls, young ladies, women, etc. on numerous, numerous occasions. There have been many a few that I have tritely labeled as "the most beautiful that I have ever seen." Never again. The luxury of having the room to loosely use that phrase is nevermore. Why? As the chin of my heart gently rests in a cupped thumb and index finger, let me tell you.

Surely, an intangible such as a person's beauty can't physically grab you. No begging to differ . . . I flat out differ. A 24-year-old goddess simply grabbed me with her beauty. Neither did I see her, nor did I hear her, but I stopped dead in my tracks, looked to my left and literally saw her attractiveness holding my left hand. Our feet set to motion and took us to the same destination: my table. She walked in front of me but sat at my table as if she knew I was sitting there. I was going to let it all go, but it was not at all possible with her sitting next to me, our knees touching, and her hand on my inner thigh.

I honestly don't know where and how to begin, so I'll just dive right in and where I land is where I land. I placed my hand on her hand and began to talk. Meanwhile, my hand was telling me of what soft skin she had. My nose was telling me of how delicious her body's scent of sensuality smelt. My ears were telling me of how sexy and voluptuous she sounded. My eyes were telling me her body language gave affirmation that her senses were talking to her in the same manner that my senses were talking to me. And all the while, my mouth was telling her of the affect her overall presence had on me.

As we talked, I watched her lips. I could only think of nibbling on them and their gloss only increased the desire. I wished that I was tasting her tongue and letting its flavor rest in the depths of my mouth. Her eyes were a gorgeous honeysuckle in color, yet icy blue, for when I gazed into them, it seemed as if my thoughts were frozen in time. Her hair was long, straight, and blonde; silky smooth as if there grew a flowing satin garment from her head. Generally, height and skin tone don't have a direct correlation. Hmmm. Her body was like the long slender meat of a banana thinly engulfed in honey with a clear coat of sex appeal. I like Honey, but only on occasion; however, I'd gladly change my name from Papa Bear to Pooh Bear.

As if hypnotized, my eyes traced the curves of her shoulders and back, along with the tips of her breasts. My hands rejoiced at the opportunity to effleurage her slim waist and thick hips. They eventually ended the motion with a cupping of the most... her butt is so rotund; I can't even begin to describe it. Her long, luscious legs, composed of supple calves and thighs, wrapped around my waist as if they were made to fit me. And attached to her ankles were soft clouds in the shape of feet.

My hands weren't alone in physically exploring the wonders of this young lady. My mouth has a story of its own to tell. My tongue had never before touch such soft lips. And my lips ... well, let's just say they made several new friends. They sweetly and gently hugged her nose, neck, shoulders, chest, belly, inner thighs, and cheeks—both sets. Even her slightly clothed genitals were a sight to see. From what I could see, she was cleanly shaved and I could literally see her smooth, bulging labia licking its lips and grinning at me. Between her body elegantly assuaging mine and her thoughts and words massaging the temples of my mind, I don't know of which I enjoyed the most. But what I do know is this: she is the most beautiful of God's creations that I have ever seen. She is sexy in every aspect of the word. Alone she stands, unmatched ... beautiful.

The Sweetest Sound (Silence)

Then . . .

An urge to speak came over me.

I sincerely wanted to catch her eye.

Not at fault, she was focused on her work

And I don't think she would have heard a cry.

As I stood and watched, my attraction grew,

But the timing was wrong and my chance was lost.

Anything beyond noticing her seemed inevitable

Until the paths of our glances happened to cross.

Upon each other, our eyes were fixed,

With a stare daring the other to melt.

She noticed me noticing her, and I ask

"Was it just me or did she feel what I just felt?"

. . . then . . . again . . .

It's inevitable for opportunities to come and go.

Reoccurrences; however, are one and few.

At hand was a second chance to leave a mark.

It came in a quick sudden. I was unprepared, too.

She had the most serious look of intrigue.
I felt as if I were a walking stone.
In reciprocity, I struck back with a look of bedroom eyes.
She was, then, tensed and I knew the feeling was, then, known.

I, then, knew what had to be done.
Nothing was the plan. Just do nothing at all.
Being aggressive at being passive is how the battle will be won.
The silent stare-downs will marinate and all silence will fall.

. . . **now.**
As if destiny were a puppeteer,
It crossed our paths once again.
Verbal love taps? Count me in. I'm ready to play.
There's no holding back this time; no time to pretend.

The silence-built wall is now eroding away.
It is silence, itself, which wears it down.
Engulfed by a new found comfort,
We are enticed by each other's sound.

There's a special felt aura within our relation.
Silently, there's a sensual connection in the works.
None the pessimist am I, but I wonder
If the aura is silenced when silence lurks?

She Does Exist
(Whoa!!!)

Life is full of marvel and grace
And its wonders come when least expected.
When life sends me **my** true wonder
I'll make sure she is truly respected.

I often thought life was a hoard,
Depriving me of my one true joy.
Life was hiding my cunning fox,
One of sensual wit and of **my** mind to toy.

Life has finally smiled upon me.
Well, it mimics my devilish grin.
She's here! Gorgeous in all with-out
With a captivating spirit lurking within.

I can hardly bear to look at her face.
My heart wants to rest upon the bed of her eyes.
Perfectly cut teeth glazed with pillowy lips,
"Can I taste of them" my mind cries.

What a joy it is to verbally embrace someone
Who takes joy in giving you loving thoughts.
One who sees the ins and outs about you
And makes you feel good for having faults.

A simple pet name has never sounded so good.
Though never was I genuinely given one before.
The way she let "honey" trickle past her plush lips
Made the walls of my sensual fortress melt to the floor.

I am not the one for being outdone,
Especially at something **I** do so well.
I've always waved the magic wand
But it is *she* that has *me* under **her** spell.

Her wand lies within her sexy brown eyes.
She says I have the twinkle of the nose.
As I kissed the softness of her tender right cheek
I could feel the twinkling of her toes.

No doubts in mind. No fears at heart.
She fits who I am to the tee.
And even if we don't grow old together,
I'll cherish what we've shared more than *merrily*.

Beauty is far more than just skin deep.
"Beautiful" was just a girl of show.
I can't fathom a word grand enough for you.
When I see and think **you**, all I can say is **whoa!**

Papa Bear . . .

Apparitionally, he's the man of the hour. Very modest in his ways, his walk, and his talk; yet, they shine outlandishly because of the unwavering confidence he places in each. Unconditionally, he's gentle and kind to all. A listener of extreme unbias is he, as well a friend to all reason and understanding. He is engulfed in integrity as if it were his skin itself. A young man blessed with wisdom beyond his years, burdened with the questions and concerns of his peers, young and old; yet, willing to share his mental treasure time after time, at any time, hence the parturition of the name Papa Bear. The personification of a gentleman and a scholar. A respecter of all persons; personable, approachable, and enjoyable to all. A tree of great stature whose roots are anchored in the soil of life, nourished by its waters of circumstance; providing shelter and shade to all that come.

... *Black Pearl* ...

The world is full of "diamonds" with qualities ranging from the splendor of The Blue Hope to the sub-parish cubic zirconium. All carry the appearance of presumed quality and value; however, the key word in the prior is "appearance." Most people aren't blessed with a well-trained eye of discernment; so, determining whether a "diamond" is fine or fagazy becomes a social task difficult within itself. One could only hope to find a jewel whose quality is not only apparent, but evident as well. That hope, for some, is reality, for they know Black Pearl. A jewel in a class of his own; a true one-and-only in regards to his quality and characteristics. A man of gentle arrogance, or confidence, for those with a distinguished eye. Like that of the Pied Piper, as he walks through life, the cohesion of his character and words play an alluring tune, often irresistible to most. In some ways, Black Pearl is like a diamond; he is not alluring to all, but none can deny that he is in a separated class of pure admiration and is highly coveted. Black Pearl, in all purity and rarity, is a showstopper. A crowd pleaser. An eye teaser. A genuine and authentic ladies' man. And on top of all that, **he knows it**.

... The Coexistence

Papa Bear—meek, modest, and respectful. Black Pearl—intentionally and extremely confident, seductive, and enticing. The description is all in the name. If you've met one of them, then you have met them both, for Papa Bear and Black Pearl are one in the same: Derrick E. Sumral. Their relationship is rather simple: where one is lacking, the other fills the void. Yet, it is complex in that when one is picking up the slack, he has to determine whether the lack there of is intentional or innocent. That enigma shines light on their differences, but brings their commonalities to the forefront as well. They, both, are very personable, with one wanting to please others and the other wanting to be pleased by others. They both always know the right things to say and/or do. The innocence of either's intentions makes it hard to tell who is at work. They both like to lie in the shadows. One doesn't prefer the luster of attention, while the other is merely waiting for that most opportune moment to step into the limelight. Their differences create their commonalities, hence creating their need for each other. They are both of magnetic force, but a magnet is not a magnet unless it has both a north and a south. The coexistence has given birth to a cursed blessing, or, maybe, a blessed curse. The cursed blessing: a sheep disguised in a fox's fur. The blessed curse: a fox disguised in sheep's wool. The coexistence: Derrick E. Sumral.

CHAPTER 6

Uncharted Waters

Nature

The sunshine giveth light for when the flower opens her eyes.

When sunshine is unbearable, the rain comes to soothe her cries.

When the wind blows, the earth grabs hold, keeping her in place.

When the world becomes cold, the earth protects her with loving grace.

To the flower, nature is comfort and is there for her every need.

But the flower, too, is oh so priceless, because nature is in need of **her** presence, indeed.

Pumpkin

Hey _____,   November 8, 2004

Uh-oh! I almost called you a special name. I've never even called my daughter's mother that name. I better be careful or I might end up getting attached. I've kind of had you on my most of the morning. Not really thinking about anything in particular for the most part, but every once in a while, I'll picture us holding each other, staring each other in the eyes, rubbing our noses together. I wish, right at this moment, I could give you a kiss. Taste your lips. Tease your tongue. I wish I were lying on my belly, face down with you lying with your bare breast on my back. I'd lie there and have you nibble, whisper, talk lightly, and giggle in my ear. Well, I have to go, but not for too long.

-Derrick

Undress

The mind's mind chooses how he is seen: naked or fully clothed.
Regardless of how he is dressed, the mind's body can't possibly be
loathed.

The chest, two mounds of clay, sculpted and glazed with beauty,
Can be lain upon like pillows or flexed to protect at the call of duty.

Arms and hands forged of steel; yet, moves with a liquidesque motion.
They are opened, wide offering comfort, shielding away all
commotion.

This body's rock hard abs are stacked like precisely placed stones.
Controlling every breath from whisper to blow, all of his sounds, all of
his tones.

Toyishlly squatting the world on his shoulders; maintaining pride and
strength.
Legs standing like towers of granite; power flowing through all their
length.

This body is adored and protected by its amber-toned skin.
It is soft and smooth to the touch and enhances all that is rough
within.

With a body physically and mentally fit, the mind is always ready to undress.

Undressing himself or the mind of another? Baring his all. Nothing more, nothing less.

Nymphony

Eager musicians anxiously waiting,
A sudden motion induces their play.
Hormones wait for that opportune moment
When auras connect and bodies sway.

Quick, light-hearted, vibrant bursts
Like the skipping strokes of a violin,
Teasing the eager of elements of pleasure;
Summoning the joys that lie within.

Rhythmic breathing and solemn whispers;
The atmosphere is sweet and mellow.
Rubs and moans flowing together
Like the movements of a lap-lying cello.

The high-pitched heights of the flute
Bounce across the room, filling the air.
Hopping atop climaxes, they prance;
Tenor and alto, they play as a pair.

Slow, deep, and strong, steady passes;
Every motion is delegated with grace.
As if watching a newborn baby in slumber,
The massaging of the soul comes from the bass.

An under-shadowing of pounding beats;
A baseline powered by the kettledrum.
The pounds are the heartbeat of the piece,
Providing the stamina for cum to cum.

The high-pitched flutters of the winds,
Melodic moans stroked by the stringed,
And the beats of the pounding percussion
Played together makes a beautiful symphony.

In the morning, the evening, or the afternoon;
At home, the office, a park, or even a concert hall;
At any given time and at any given place,
The sounds of our song make passionate nymphony.

Why You So Soon

To me, you are not too soon. However, you **are** early. Early in that I **did** expect to find you, but not just yet. But I am overjoyed, to say the least. I'd rather you be early than be late. I do understand why you would think it is too soon. But you must understand that I have pondered on and questioned my needs, wants, desires, and preferences and I have no doubt in my mind about who and what I want in a woman.

I need affection. I need someone that will show me, in some way, shape, or form, that I mean something to them. I need someone who is honest. Not brash, but sincerely truthful. I need someone who will be my companion in life: in the good and the bad. I need a friend.

I want someone who I can talk to. I want someone who can talk to me as well. I want someone who I can joke and laugh with. I want someone who I can be myself around and who feels comfortable being herself around me. I want someone who respects and has an understanding of the significance of GOD in my life. I want someone who wants me for me.

I desire a nympho; not just physically, but mentally and emotionally as well. I desire someone who, with just a simple look, can turn me on and be turned on herself. I desire someone who thinks anytime is the right time to make love. Mind you, making love is not always of the physical realm. Case in point, I desire someone who feels her mind is being made love to as she reads this at this very moment. I desire someone who will make love me with her voice, her thoughts, . . . her words. I desire a sexy, passionate nympho; one who will excessively make love to me: body, soul, and spirit.

I prefer someone who is beautiful and has something about her beauty that sets it apart from anyone else's (e.g., freckles). I prefer someone who would have to look up slightly in order to kiss my lips. I prefer someone with lovely hair. I prefer someone with ample breasts and a pretty ass. I prefer someone who is comfortable with her body and her person. I prefer someone who can turn me on from me just thinking about her. I prefer someone with soft skin and sexy lips. Most of all, I prefer someone with gorgeous eyes. Eyes that can see and believe that I want her.

Man of Steel

Scars, blemishes, deformities:
A collection of life's battle wounds.
The world has schemed and attacked,
But I'm not piped by its sorrowful tunes.

I've taken a many of blows and punches.
I've been shot at and still escaped.
I've even been taken by surprise by a girl,
Shamefully, damn near raped.

I've had my father turn his back on me.
To make matters worse, it's happened twice.
My guard is up in regards to trusting people.
The blood in my veins is as cold as ice.

I thought I found my superwoman:
A heroine alongside her hero.
But her costume was just for pretend:
Dress-up for a dressed-down zero.

Then there are the punk-ass motherfucka's
That claim to be your "boys," your friends.

Yet, they, too, turn and stick you in the ass,
But my dignity my pride defends.

My mind and my heart fight back-and-forth,
Quarreling over who is the mightiest,
When my spirit man quietly steps in
And nonchalantly states he's the tidiest.

My mind is tops. My game is superior.
I provide whatever my "friendships" need.
My soil is strong enough to support a Sequoia.
And you know what?! I'll even plant the seed.

Directly and indirectly, challenges come,
But the champ remains undaunted, standing tall.
Neither praises nor hexes can bring me down.
I will never again let my mind and heart fall.

Then came a honeysuckle lily.
Her stem drank from my heart's brook.
Her petals ate of my mind's sunshine,
While her roots flipped through my defense's book.

My fortress of strength has been tranquilized.
My defenses just would not deploy,
When she gave me the sweetest, most gentle kiss
That produced the single, most strongest tear of joy.

Stalked

Deep down, everyone wants to be crazily adored.
Wanting to be a person's deepest desire, never being ignored.

To receive unceasing attention is flattery at its best.
Your heart melts knowing that, in you, one desires to nest.

The world seems to be yours because you are gravely craved.
Your every word can be repeated and every memory has been saved.

Eventually, the mind becomes tired and the heart becomes weary.
The admirer overbears, and of their attention, you become leery.

Grateful in the beginning, you are now in need of space.
From adored to stalked; they're following you from place to place.

No matter what you do they tend to know your every motion.
They're there even when you find a friend to help you through the
commotion.

This stalker has friends as well, and they smile in your face, too.

But like words in the wind, they drift away and there's nothing you can do.

Unfortunately, one cannot choose who their admirers will be.

I wish I had the power to choose, for it is loneliness that is stalking me.

When Nothing Matters

When no one can say a word that will move your spirit,
The song of life still plays, only you don't hear it.

When the sweetest taste is bland and the sourest is the same,
The flavors of life beckon; you answer not, as if you have no name.

Arousing aromas prance by; they stir neither a nudge nor a smile,
The scent of danger does not move you; your awareness is on trial.

Regardless of context, circumstances seem to just not be.
Life moves all around, but you, you could care less to see.

The touches from the world go unfelt; all nerves have gone numb.
Nothing seems to move you even though you're not deaf, blind, or dumb.

Your mind has stalled and its thoughts no longer gain ground.
Your heart has become asylumed; not a feeling can be found.

But there is that time when you **are** touched and when you **are** moved.

There's no arguing the feeling, for there's a passion your heart has proved.

That time is the very moment you feel your heart's pitter-patters;
When she is all you feel is when nothing else even matters.

Blackjack
(The Gambler)

The game is of second nature.
It is only natural for him to play.
His participation is not intentional,
But his play is what makes his day.

Inevitably his cards are **given** to him
And he never knows what he'll get.
But he has to work with what is given
So he strategically places his bets.

With a bad hand, he has no choice.
He asks for help card by card.
His hand can be so undesirable,
Making his decision to play at all very hard.

At times, the gambler gets lucky.
The winning cards just fall in place.
Needing not of the dealer's trickeries,
He has, preferably, the King and its Ace.

Sometimes he gets a double card hand.
He plays them both. It's called a split.
Why he risks a two-for-one is simple:
You never know if one of them will split.

The mediocre hand is, by far, the scariest.
Does he need more cards or just stay put?
He could be greedy for prideful glory
Or foolishly shoot himself in the foot.

Winning a hand is a bittersweet moment.
Should he stop playing or be dealt in again?
The gambler's greed will never let him stop.
The whole point of playing is to get a bigger win.

The gambler's play will never be done.
Handing out numerous defeats is his goal.
Keep in mind the dealer is a gambler too,
Except the cards are under his control.

Chips Ahoy

Before I even had a chance to speak, you detoured my bloodline.

You knew I had a strike, and having nowhere to lean, you took my wall.

You even did it again, with a substitute, hoping for a flat line.

As if you hadn't done enough, you're still demising my manhood's fall.

I had a daughter **and** a wife and, in that, I took much pride.

You corrupted hearts, minds, and feelings, bring the family to shame.

You despicably use people and behind their faces, you laugh and hide.

You stole my family, bitch! I hate the very sound of your name.

You stir up the troubles of "others," but only after I get involved.

When I think I have something good, all you do is show the bad.

Your deceit is such a tasteless way to show how your tactics have evolved.

Your spoiling of my joy with others has become annoying, just a tad.

What have I done that hasn't already warranted a repercussion?

Why don't you be a man and answer me face-to-face?

Why the hell are we even having this discussion?!

Why the fuck are you on my back!?! Get yo' punk ass out of my space!!!

Why are you such a coward? Don't you know how to play fair?

When I throw rocks, you use stones. When I throw stones, you use boulders.

I'm tired and playtime's over. I'm returning to you your evil glare.

I'm well beyond being pissed off. I have chips on **both** shoulders.

Just A Taste

I never thought I would find that "one" again,

Until I found a potential companion & lover, and, always, a friend.

But, all I got was just a taste.

She exemplifies the true essence of woman, with dignity and with grace.

With arms open wide, our hearts and minds simply fell into place.

However, all I got was just a taste.

Body of a goddess: from the hairs on her head to the nails on her toes;

Her enchanting brown eyes, moist soft lips, even the freckles on her nose.

And all I got was just a taste.

I'm a hungry man yearning for his heart's desire.

She's the most body-chilling angel who has the heat to light my fire.

And all I get is just a taste?

In a matter of no time, her spirit *captured* my soul.

She is the piece that is missing; the "one" to make me whole.

And all it took was just a taste.

Chapter 7

The Elements' Cataclysms

Really?

That wink. That glare. That gaze. That stare.

That look given to drop panties to the floor.

After you get her, would you give the same looks once more?

That word. That phrase. That seductive line.

Those words spoken to ensure **you** don't lose.

You've won her heart. Now, those same words, would you reuse?

That brush. That rub. That squeeze. That touch.

The touch that was received at its spoken demand.

When she's ready for more, will you use the same hand?

That compliment. That song. Maybe, even that poem.

Those sentimental deeds used to "seal the deal."

Were they just something extra or were they truly for real?

One-time wows and wonders are easy to do.

The things one does to obtain one's gain.

But after one obtains, would one remain the same to retain?

That Word . . .

…is the creation of creation: the beginning of it all.

…is the reason why there is falter and why everything will fall.

…can create in you a certain patience, a desire to stay sane.

…can create in you a certain fire, a fury that you cannot tame.

…can instantaneously freeze one's everything,

producing truces, stalemates, and cease-fires.

…can turn a heart of gold into a heart of stone

and turn the most honest into the worst of liars.

…will bend you over backwards so that you'll rise in the clutch.

…will bend you over forwards and sodomize your Dutch.

…is therapeutic to the soul, soothing all aches and pains.

…is detrimental to one's well-being, with all its strife and strains.

…could be someone's entrance, to a world of joy and glee.

…could be someone's exit, allowing the imprisoned to be let free.

…can produce butterflies with no metamorphosis needed.

…cannot be mistaken when present, regardless if it's denied or pleaded.

…will gingerly lay you flat and rub down your body
all to backstab you, watch you bleed, and then smile.

…will flush the toilet in the middle of a life's warm shower
and then, in the time of need, walk the extra mile.

…is like that of a saint: a blessing to one and all.
…is like that of the dickens: yearning to *help* one fall.

…could be a doctor, counted on for special healing;
expected to meet the needs of others, no matter how it's feeling.

…could be a villain, notorious for its bad;
spoiling whatever it pleases, in spite of all its clad.

…possesses a viper's venom. In a word: deadly.
…is the song that charms the viper. It **is** the medley.

…will gather all its stress, worries, hurts, and sorrows
and snuggle and cuddle them across your chest.

…will ease your mind of your daily burdens
like ice melting in between her breasts.

...will discreetly nourish you like a morning's dew
and answer unasked questions as if it already knew.

...will whisper in your ear and make you close your eyes.
...speak outlandishly, deterring the dumb **and** the wise.

...is used ever so loosely; watered down, having no flavor.
...has a taste so rich, it is cherished beyond a simple savor.

...will ask for nothing but will squeeze from you all of your time.
...will ask for a penny and expect you to give a dime.

...will lick its lips and give you the sweetest kiss.
...will turn away with a shoulder colder than the Swiss.

...will sneak up on you while you are "sleep"
and consume your every breath and thought.

...may very well be mankind's universal language;
sweet-talking all, stealing their hearts—never being caught.

...will never, ever, play fair and there is nothing you can do.
...doesn't really care, so how you embrace it is entirely up to you.

Daylight Savings

Mistakes could be corrected,
Memories could be erased.
OR
Mistakes could be avoided,
Memories could be replaced.

The past could be edited,
The future could be elapsed.
OR
The present can be arranged,
Allowing a mutual medium, perhaps.

A retract of time gone by,
Trading what is for what might.
OR
A preterition of schedule,
Allowing youth to catch up and possibly unite.

The Cumuli

Just floating, carelessly drifting;

Endless thoughts of you on my mind;

None of this even seems real; however,

Somehow, someway, I've reached cloud nine.

Cloud eight had to be when I realized

That my desires were only for you, too.

Cloud seven was when I realized

A serious desire for me lied within you.

Total enchantment is the name of cloud six.

Staring into your eyes took me there.

A simple touch took me to cloud five.

There, of semi-solid feelings I became aware.

I stood at the open door of cloud four.

Your voice invited me in.

I think you wanted to share cloud three.

I could see it in your glance's grin.

What to do, I knew not; stumped at cloud two.

Stunned by the vision of you in my right eye.

Cloud one hit quick. Is it even in the air?

It was your presence as you walked by.

I've just brought you backwards

From where I want to be to where I am now.

Is it **you** who'll take me forwards

And, without this recollection, remember how?

Right (Write) 'On, Nigga! (Why I Write)

Sometimes to display grammatical excellence.

And, at times, using my linguistical twang.

There's no particular reason why I write.

Plain and simple: writing is just my thang.

The pad is, no doubt, the best listener,

And I can tell it whatever the hell I want.

Regardless of content, my voice is heard.

There's no need for hiding, no need to taunt.

I've had some question my purpose,

Suggesting that I'm trying to please a broad.

Most times, they are pleased themselves.

Am I alone, or do you, too, find that to be ironically odd?

I write to let the truth be told.

No room for guessing; no questions needed to be asked.

Though my wordplay calls for no simplicity,

It is the truth; no matter how it is masked.

What is written is what is meant:
Words in its purest; no cultivation.
What is written is untouched.
Words in its cleanest; no adulteration.

Writing is my self-maintenance.
It is how I stay in tune with myself.
It is my mental and spiritual treasure.
It is my wealth beyond all wealth.

My love for silence makes it hard to speak
And my thoughts hang around like there is no time.
Spontaneously, my pencil impatiently whispers.
There is no better way for me to ease my mind.

Words can be twisted, misconstrued, and chopped,
Omitted, edited, misquoted, ignored, and broken.
I write when I have something notable to say
And when words are better off said unspoken.

Some say spoken words will make me look bigga'.
Well, these are **my** words. How do **you** figga'?
Silence is a thought's true grave digga'.
My words speak volumes. Write on, lil' nigga!
Right 'on!

Sunshine

Have you wondered if you'll ever find that place
Where it seemed as if the sun always shined?
That place, when growing up, you were always told
Was just a small, imaginary place in your mind.

No disrespect to those who think they know,
But everyone has that place and seeing it may seem gray.
It's not difficult to find. It is simply that place
Where one ray of sunshine always brightens your day.

If **I** ever *seeked* to sneak a peek,
Then any sacrifices would be worth their while.
Delighted, discouraged, happy, or sad:
Uplifted, am I, in that place called your smile.

Vitamin B

Once, a pure and perfectly healthy "body"
With a cough or sneeze from now to then.
My body, always noticing the "viral infections" of others,
Has been overcome by a congestion it does not comprehend.

Naturally, the body fights back with every defense:
Internally: vitamins and minerals; externally: a coat.
In most cases, the body wins out with no help needed.
However, this battle is long-lived and I need the antidote.

Conventional *medicine* does not hinder this congestion.
I need something genuine, maybe some charisma and charm,
Or, maybe comforting thoughts passing through gorgeous eyes,
Or, just some sensual *friendship* to distract this bodily harm.

It is said that an illness can be cured with kindness and affection,
Making it possible for a wink, maybe a smile, to be my cure.
One could only dream of a healing kiss from glossy lips;
A combination of it all would definitely clear me up, I'm sure!

This *build-up* needs a soft-skinned touch, a warm embrace.

This case won't be cured by any medicine, serum, or warm teacup.

I can't complain too much since I purposely withhold the buildup.

No big fan of liquor, but maybe a shot of Brandy will help me speak up.

At times, I reflect on the numerous tried remedies of old:

All that would, could, should, didn't, or, somewhat help me.

Often, I turn full circle with one particular solution in mind,

Hesitant, but, yet, hungry for a massive dose of Vitamin B.

Indoor Rain

I cry because life was created for a **greater good**.
…then, because life's meaning is misunderstood.

I cry for those, in **life**, who did all that they could've.
…then, for those who'll, in the end, wish they would've.

I cry because **life** can be made out of what you know.
Yet, some won't make it because they'll never know.

I cry for joy because of echoing laughter.
…then, in pain because of the reasoning after.

I cry at the sight of beauty since I like to watch.
…then, for beauty's bite can make you turn to Scotch.

I cry because love can be seen, felt, smelt, and heard.
Then, I cry, for "love" is my most hated word.

I cry because love was once synonymous to "D".
…now, because my heart will no longer let that be.

Sometimes I open up and have a "someone" in sight.
I cry, for it feels good and for wondering if it is right.

I cry because **my** person seems to be walking free.
But, he is locked away, alone, and no one has the key.

I seldom cry through my eyes. In that, I find no gain.
But my heart and mind wear coats due to my indoor rain.

I cry a single tear for joy and a single tear for pain.
Yet, only a single tear will drop, for the two are one in the same.

Shut Up

For those who have nothing else better to do
Than worry about what I do when it don't involve you:
You seem to always knows the purpose of my strolls,
I don't see the soles of my feet, so tell me how's the view.

For those who always got suh'em shitty to say,
But catch a case of lockjaw when I come they way:
You niggas, hoes, bros, keep your fucking mouth closed.
I didn't raise my hand for these silly games to play.

For those who speak on things as if they always knew,
But really they don't know, they're just hoping it's true:
I don't mean to bust ya bubble, but here's suh'em fo' ya trouble:
Y'all stupid motherfuckahs can shut the fuck up, too!

For those who say they're brave and wanna explore,
But get overwhelmed or uneasy when I answer the door:
If you're scared of the game, then keep your *mouths* tamed.
It's no inconvenience to start over. I done dunnit before.

For those who shall read this and feel I'm talkin' 'bout you,
With a guilty conscience thinking "I'm hopin' he through":
I'm a little tired of being pissed, so, I'll grant you your wish,
I'll use my words another time 'cuz they're a valuable few.

What Is It? . . . Again!

Is it coincidence?
I already knew her name and knew her face.
I never thought I'd give her presence an embrace.

Is it her face?
I usually try not to focus on the source of my demise,
But she has the face of a goddess. Sexy smile. Lovely eyes.

Is it her body?
She has an attractively proportioned body. Quite statuesque.
From her back and her thighs to her feet and her breasts.

Is it her voice?
A voice so soft and warm; in it, I'd place my mind to nest.
A sultry sound that lullabied my heart and soul to rest.

Is it her mind?
Her mind, though not seen, proved to have all power and might.
The words she chose to speak kept our conversations in flight.

Is it her touch?

We had a short holding of hands that literally made me melt.

My hand is now priceless, for an angel I have felt.

Is it the taste?

As I held her hand, I kissed it. Goodbye until we next meet.

After the kiss, I licked my lips. I knew not salt to taste so sweet.

Is it her presence?

Her existence alone makes me ponder how 1+1 can equal 3.

A road short or long matters not. Maybe she + I can equal we.

It is everything!

Everything that I know of her is everything that I want to please.

To Life: If she is not the one for me, then it is not nice to taunt & tease.

A Daughter's Touch

With all femininity and masculinity aside, a man is simply just that—a man, as in mankind. A man made in the image of God. An earthly image of God made to worship him. It is safe to say that God, himself, desired to be "touched." Respectively, man desires to be "touched" as well. Naturally, man desires to be touched by woman and woman desires to be touched by man. Being a man myself, I wholeheartedly believe God's greatest creation is woman, and her touch is a delightful phenomenon. And as great as a woman's touch is, it is not the greatest earthly touch there is.

That hand is only a small replication of yours, yet its touch epitomizes love. Such a small hand but such a big heart. The touch from her hand, in an instant, brings overwhelming joy. Pride and integrity has no choice but to form a glowing shield about your chest. The touch from that small hand tells you there is no problem worth worrying about. A kiss from those little lips wipes away all pain and places a seal of guarantee wherever they touch. The hugs from outstretched arms do not completely circumference the body but the genuine feeling can engulf the globe. One could think that a breath is simply a small deposit of oxygen to the body, but one would be wrong. That breath causes a rise and fall of a belly and chest that deposits a tranquil peace, looking as if it were floating atop a wave in the ocean as she lies across your chest.

As if it weren't enough, the "touch" goes beyond the physical. The soft and sweet voice stops every step, pauses every thought, and halts every feeling, beckoning and receiving the attention of your every avenue. Her smile is like an upside-down rainbow with two fluffy clouds, beaming brightly with every possible color, touching you as if you were the pot of gold. The worth of that pot of gold could not buy the least of the feelings induced by her touch: a daughter's touch. The most rewarding and immaculate "touch" is one that will never ever be able to be described by words. The spontaneous, unprovoked "I love you, Daddy": enough said.

11.30.2004

Lupercalia

A day full of endearment,
Every word is perfectly chosen.
Whispered sweet nothings in the air;
In that day you wish you were frozen.

A day full of compassion,
Every thought is about the joy *they* bring.
Memories fill your mind with vibrant color;
A day that makes your spirit sing.

A day full of wonder,
Every feeling seems to be unreal.
Curious about what "it" is that they do;
The only unquestioned is how you feel.

A day full of passion,
Every touch is precisely placed.
Passion's energy is overwhelming;
Every touch, even a bite, has grace.

A day full of sincerity,
Differences cease to cause dissention.
Cons aren't overlooked but understood,
While pros assuage all attention.

A day full of the expected unexpected,
Surprises come somehow, someway.
This time is ultimately expected to pass;
A time desired to be every day.

Full Bloom

Absolute natural beauty;
Life's purest token of affection.
In a vast valley of weeds,
Nature has her pruned to perfection.

Robust, voluptuous lips,
Like peach roses in full bloom;
A smile that brightens my every day
Like sunny rays in early June.

Beautiful, round eyes,
Like rose petals in a bed.
The stare is sturdy and the gaze is soft-
A place to rest my soul's head.

A fragrance of sensuality;
This sweet smell is her voice.
A sound accented with distinct charm,
Drawing one nigh without choice.

From gray thunderstorms to blazing heat,

A tranquil breeze to a pitch-black noon,

Her existence alone fairs my weather,

For she's a never-ending, gorgeous full bloom.

Just Wait

My Dear Lady,

For quite some time I've been encountering "things" about my person that is not of the norm and they have raised questions within myself **and** others. I spent even more time staring in a *mirror* in effort to know myself. Hence, I know my heroics. I know of all my shortcomings. I know my likes and my dislikes, my tendencies and limitations, my tempters and those who repulse me. I can easily say that I know who I am, fully. Well, at least, I thought I did. I anxiously pace back and forth, yearning to know you and wanting you to know me and, at times, I've walked past that *mirror* and have had to stop; unfamiliar with "who" I was seeing. After seeing this *unfamiliar me* on a regular basis, I decided to, once again, take another deep stare. I noticed several pleasing but questionable "things."

My walk is more confident as if I have something extraordinarily special to be proud of. I've always held my head high, but I now make sure that my surroundings are as perfect as they could possibly be. My thoughts have remained the same; however, my approach to thinking has broadened, as if I am looking through another's eyes, thinking with another's mind. My "eyes" search deep for something more than what is initially seen. Why?

For you. Simply, for you. As I stared in the *mirror*, I noticed a part of me that not even I, myself, knew. And this part of me thought, spoke, and acted as if he weren't alone, yet, he was. It was all in preparation for you. The world ought to know how proud I am to have you as my lady when it, and it will, becomes gospel. My feelings and emotions have been preparing to be more understanding, realizing that your thoughts will be just as, if not more, important as my thoughts. My "eyes" search for every drop of beauty that they can find. I won't lie and say that beauty is not important to me, because it is. However, my "eyes" have found that beauty is more than an outward appearance and no longer do they find satisfaction from the physicalities of beauty alone. I find myself searching for wisdom. Knowledge. Intellect. Confidence. Humility. Sense of humor. Compassion. **You.**

Patiently waiting,

Derrick E. Sumral

Now or Later

Right now hovers an ever-present gray.

I stand, not confused of what, but how;

My desire is known, and for *it* daily I pray.

I wish to stop everything and have *it* now.

"*It* shall be yours, my son" is what I hear Him say.

It is not an it: "it" is the woman that I crave.

A craving that struck when we first laid eyes on we.

Scared to lose before gaining—right now, be brave.

Whether now or later, I'll have to give; nothing is free.

And whatever the road to her heart is, I'll happily pave.

Now or later is never never, and for her I truly feel.

Of my total person I want to give, no regard to wealth.

A letter written for her, only she should break my seal.

My desire for her is a passion, my sickness and my health.

Right now, I just want her. Later, can come the *kneel*.

The dead end road. A journey we both share.

And I must admit, my later looks to be far from now.

She might want to rest; for a new man, she may not care.

My now may be later; to that, I objectionately raise my brow.

If later is the storm, then the worst of weather I'll fair.

Can't Wait

I don't have to hear those three words **all** the time,
But I can't wait until they become your words of choice.
The talk, long or short, makes no difference.
All I want is to hear your voice.

Any holds there are, are done with caution.
I can't wait to freely touch you hand to hand.
A time of physical freedom for you as well,
All I want is your touch; wherever it may land.

Sweet dreams should be followed by precious reality.
And I can't wait to gaze upon your face every morn.
Kiss your cheek in hope to look into your eyes,
The very place where true feelings are sworn.

Your lips' movement is like silk in the wind.
I can't wait to free the urges my feelings compile.
My every depression can be wiped away.
All I need is your beautiful smile.

I don't want to wait to share my self with you,

Creating a union just as deep as kinship.

But **I WILL** wait in order to do things correctly.

All I want is your genuine and honest friendship.

Always There

A thought of you in the midst of mayhem settles all dissention.
In tranquil serenity, visual memories assuage my attention.

In my first victory in the battle of love, you were by my side.
When love got the best of me, unknowingly, you upheld my pride.

When woeful times hover gray, you shine a brighter light.
Your aura is always near when the wings of joyous times take flight.

At times of loneliness, I'm accompanied by your soft, sweet voice.
Every other thought leaves and squanders as if they had no choice.

This poem is an unfinished poem. It is the **only** poem that I have not been able to finish. I wrote the first half of this poem in the Spring of 2004. I could not finish. I wrote the second half in the Summer of 2006. I could not finish. Not being able to finish a poem was frustrating and I almost attempted to force myself to finish it. It is, now, Spring of 2011 and I have realized that I will not be able to finish this poem. I don't believe in "Always There." Not for me, anyways. I cannot truthfully write about something that I don't believe in ...

Obviously, at one point in time, I **did** believe in "Always There." From this page forward, you will experience why I do not believe anymore ...

Rock or Hard Place?

Rock: a *concreted mass* of *stony* material. Concreted: combined, blended, or solidified into a solid mass. Mass: a quantity or aggregate of matter usually of considerable size. Stony: having the nature of a concretion of earthy material. Hence, rock: a big and heavy piece of shit that is pretty much useless. When something is mentioned, it is usually because, in some fashion, it helps you or it hurts you. In most cases, rocks usually get in the way. With a rock being big and heavy, one would think to just move around it. What if the rock had you pinned in some way? You want to move it, but you can't. It is too big to simply grab a hold of it and move it. Even if you could grab it, it's too damn heavy to move once you do. So, you just exist, experiencing what pain there is. You may ... or may not, seek the "help" of others. Some try. Some just look, see the rock, and then pretend not to see the rock ... or you. Knowing you have no help, from others or yourself, you still struggle. You squirm. You strain. You push. You fight. Why? Because you can still see. You see past the rock and notice life is ongoing. You see all of the "rock-less" motha'fucka's walking around doing whateva' they want. Some are looking at you. Some laugh.

Some point fingers and make faces. This is fucked up: some even try to cast more rocks on top of the big ass rock you already have. What the hell you gon' do?

Hard: not easily penetrated; difficult to bear. Place: physical environment or surrounding; space, atmosphere; a particular part of a surface or body. Hard place: an atmosphere of hardship, difficulty, or pain, antagonized by rancor or bitterness. Fuck that.

Hard place: something that pisses you off and makes you want to knock somebody the fuck out, regardless of who the fuck they are, even yourself. I found that hard places are pretty much anything, except the future. The future can always be penetrated. The penetration depends on decisions made in the present. Sometimes the present cannot be penetrated easily because some decisions can be very difficult. And the past…it simply can't be penetrated. It is already done. There is nothing that can be done or said that can change the past. And the past is where most hard places come from. The past is always pushing you forward whether you want it to or not. You can't go back. It is done. And you can't penetrate it to un-do it. Hard places haunt you. They are always lurking over your shoulder. Looking into your present. Whispering in your ear. Mocking you. Teasing you. Antagonizing you. Always bringing up old shit. Just shut the fuck up!

I don't know which one is worse: the rock . . . or the hard place. The rock is big and heavy, pretty much unmovable. You're not strong enough to move it and nobody else can help because they ain't no stronger than you are. The hard place will not move, won't be moved and is always at your back; the one place your eyes cannot see but only know is there. They both tease you. The rock gets in your way and lets you see past it; however, it knows it is too heavy a matter for you to handle, so, it just sits there. The hard place holds up its index and middle fingers and waves them behind your head. People see them and laugh, but you have no clue *what* they're laughing at but you know something is there. Of the two, there is one thing that is worse: being between a rock **and** a hard place—in a difficult or uncomfortable position with no attractive way out. Better stated: You're fucked! I honestly don't know of any attractive ways *out*. I'm tired and weary from foolin' with my rocks and hard places. I'll just focus on the attractive ways *in*. Why not? I don't have nothing else to lose. I'm already stuck.

Lucky's Charms

I, my *modest* self, call myself "Lucky"
While everybody else has their own name for me.
They see the hoppin', skippin' & pseudo-pimpin'
But it's my "charms" that cause *them* not to trust me.

Sweet nothings skip through the air like *shooting stars;*
Usually, pondered from spontaneous, quick wit.
Words with slyness that makes you play them thrice over.
Things said that make you wonder if men are really from Mars.

To reach the stars, there's the ride on the *red balloon.*
A quiet, peaceful journey in a basket of whatever pleases.
A basket woven together with whatever *it* is that teases.
Never mind the later, all you know is you want *it* soon.

The ride takes you to the *blue moons* that rest in the skies.
Their soft stare lullabies to sleep, and drifts, your spirit nigh.
But that certain glance can cause a trance. Check your thigh.
Only magic can explain why there is blue in brown eyes.

Curling over the moons, a *rainbow* reaches out to its "earth."

Numerous colors, usually, paints a confusing, un-pretty painting,

But the placement of these hues is unexplainably remarkable.

The rainbow's "colors" are quite intangible, so what's its worth?

At the end of the rainbow, a *pot of gold* waits for its taking.

A stunning pot full of shiny "coins" waiting to be spent.

Happily tired from lifting the heavy pot, you lie down to rest.

There's a slight urge to scratch a skin slightly itching … aching.

The "sensation" comes from the foliage: a field of a *green clover*.

Green: the color of envy and of the clovers that make you "itch."

It's mind over matter and "itches" fade away. No kids. No Trix.

Besides, you notice the ground around you and know it's not over.

Around the pot and in the clovers are imprints of *purple horseshoes*.

Majestic and beautiful steps of a horse, but a horse you are not.

You realize the imprints are signs of luck, so you continue to trot.

A spirit riding like the wind in a one-man race. No way to lose.

"Lucky" can only take pride in your pursuit of his *pink heart*.

However, some "pursuits" are unlucky and innocently go unnoticed.

There's a preoccupation of keeping his "charms" in correct order.

This preservation is the reason for your racing pursuit from the start.

Ahead of the race, there's "Lucky" and after him, *they* take aim.

There are times when he evades and others when he stands still.

All the while his "charms" spill and fill his aura in great abundance.

Charms that ever so greatly personifies his "lucky" name.

CHAPTER 8

The Oasis

Which Is It?
(Either Way . . .)

It is said that a smile can speak a thousand words.

Stealthily, there are conjunctions and contradictions that lie within.

That smile is so beautiful that you see nothing else.

But those words mumble messages you've yet to comprehend.

It is said that one's eyes are the doorway to their soul.

The ginger "smile" of a twinkled eye receives just that in return.

Souls mate instinctively—the mirrored reflection of an eye.

Mumble not, but murmur. "One thousand words" voice their concern.

It is said that one's touch shows the sincerity of their heart.

The "smile" from un-lonely skin has a "thousand"-strong stand.

If smiles bring awareness and eyes "open," then a touch must "seal."

A touch is true but ever-changing; like footprints in the sand.

Smiles, winks, and touches could very well mean hope for the future.

Unfortunately, the "thousand words" always seem to be retroactive.

The aromas of auras breath life; concurrently, exuding the smell of death.

Which is *it*: attractively unattractive or unattractively attractive?

Breathe

My Dear Lady,

Besides a heartbeat, there's one thing that everyone who has ever lived has shared in common. Not everyone has heard. Not everyone has touched. Neither seen. Nor spoken. But there's one sense that I've left untouched but never goes untouched: smell. And to smell, one has to breathe. Breaths come a million in a day: highly overlooked and highly taken for granted. Granted, there are some people whose every breath comes a little more difficult than others. They cherish every breath they have, but, in general, a breath is nothing more than just that ... a breath. God, with his almighty hand, took dirt and made man in his own image. But it wasn't until God breathed into mans' lungs for the man to have life. Every living creature has to breathe in order to live. Man, woman, boy, and girl. All animals of the land, birds of the air, and fish of the sea. A rose. The queen of all flowers. The queen of all plants. But a rose is just that—a plant. No lungs. No nose. Yet, it still needs a breath of air in order to live. Now, not by any means am I close to being a rose. Neither am I close to receiving the reverence and respect that its presence alone does. However, I want, need, like, and love to breathe. But, for me, a breath is more than just an intake of an accumulation of air molecules. For me, a breath is a smile.

A smile that welcomes. A smile that dawns sunshine into my day. For me, a breath is a vision. A visualization of having that smile in my life every day. For me, a breath is a touch. Hug me; kiss me ... with your mind, heart and body. For me, a breath is a voice.

That sweet, sweet sound that keeps me "awake" while I sleep. For me, a breath is you. And at every breath, the "life" within my "body" is once again renewed. And from now until my last, I desire to breathe heavily, with every breath being a breath of you.

Never holding my breath,

Derrick E. Sumral

Euphoric Lovely Excellence

Every inch of every curve is sculpted to perfection,
Like milk and honey is love's illustrious complexion.

Aphrodisiacesque is every thought to comprehend
Impassionate words that flow like silk in the wind.

Nigh draws all heed to every aspect of love's person;
All to make my every desire for love to worsen.

Eternity whispers for a celestial union in paradise,
Pardoning selfishness with a coup de gras in sacrifice.

Passionately, sweet love's excellence is a lull-ish song.
Sensuous in all her ways, for her, I'll forever long.

Slitheran

Atop of Warriors Circle resides the spot of all spots.
Inside, a Circle of Warriors; linked, initiated by shots.

After shots drop, tags hang engraved with your letterin'
A rookie no more, unconsciously ranked up to veteran.

All separate agendas aside, every movement is slitheran.
All beef aside, there's a brother's trust: love not witherin'.

Get free spirited with beats bangin' and catch a freestyle verse.
Step out with charisma danglin' and catch a penile purse.

A house of show-how, assuaging dames like street Casanova.
A house of know-how, the street equipped for corporate takeova'.

Getting and staying lit is the Circle's primary objective.
On top of that, get blazed to keep life's pleasures in perspective.

This house has personal invite, so, whatever you do
Don't make haste in choosing the house. The house will choose you.

A. P. B.

All and any. Every … that has a mouth to speak.
Those that can look with intentions to take.
None to plenty. No one to everyone—listen here.
Especially for those serious, and even those fake.

Persons and people. All beings living life.
Men acknowledged, overlooked, and unknown.
Domestics, nomads—possessing mind, body, and spirit.
Mankind in general; newborn to full-grown.

Beware and be warned. Talk null and listen heavy.
Pay attention to caution and to warning, take heed.
The ground is not of eggshells, but do tread lightly.
Compliance isn't a must, but understanding should be agreed.

Companions are chosen. Choosing takes thought.
A.P.B. aside, I chose for me. Nothing against you.
At times, choices overlap. Troubles may arise.
Overlapping my choice may not be the best thing to do.

Morning Sickness

Unimaginable … indescribable …
Wakening … gut wrenching pain

Unexplainable body heat
Abnormal beads of sweat, more like rain

Groggy and well beyond tired
A dark fog for brains … concrete for feet

Skin moist and clammy
The air … brisk and cold like sleet

No single remedy
Neither is one reliable

Sickness only you feel
But others see that it's undeniable

Control Burning

...A cool breeze brushes by.
The grass is green. The grass is lush.
The beauty of the waving blades
Matched only by the surrounding hush.

Time passes by and seasons change.
If "grass" were its own, "it" would be suffice.
Unfortunately, the grass is of the "Earth"
And "others" of the Earth make grass pay a price.

The grass ... hungry and thirsty,
Seemingly dead due to the world's ways,
Has a caretaker watching by the wayside.
Strategically, he sets the grass ablaze.

The grass lies there scorched.
Blackened beyond recognition.
The grass doesn't, but the Earth does know
The grass is being reconditioned.

With revengeful stealth, the "green" is back.

The grass ... no longer parched or dry;

The beauty displayed is greater than before ...

A cool breeze brushes by ...

Black & White

White . . . often paralleled with light. Light . . . often paralleled with revelation . . . definition . . . "a stroke of brilliance". The light allows you to see what lies ahead and what lurks around. Light gives the mind a sense of certainty. The mind believes what is seen through the eye. Light allows for graceful and steadfast movement. Avoiding risk and embracing guarantee is made simplistic. The brainstorming of an approach, in essence, is unnecessary due to light giving opportunity of foreseeing a viable path. Light . . . the natural guide of life. Have you seen the light? . . . .

Black . . . often paralleled with dark. Dark . . . often paralleled with disarray . . . inconsistency . . . "in a state of confusion". Darkness does not allow you to see anything near **or** far, and sometimes, it doesn't allow you to see yourself. Darkness gives the mind a sense of uncertainty. The mind does not know in who or what to trust. How can it? It cannot see who or what it is supposed to be trusting. But does it need to? Sifting through darkness calls for stealthy movements, and sometimes, dormancy. In the dark, the mind stands still. Every movement has the potential of being a risk . . . or a guarantee . . . .

. . . . . . .At this juncture, the unconsciously naïve mindset of man, in general, would proclaim light to be the greater of the two, **but, oh contraire!** This is where light becomes a crutch, crippling the mind, causing it to stumble into consensus, conformity, and normality. Though, a scary place it may be, the darkness is a safe haven. Yes, indeed, it is hard to *see* in the dark. But, conversely, in the dark, it is hard to be seen. Darkness gives "room" for the mind to stretch. Stretching is vital for growth. Take stretching a muscle for example. When you stretch a muscle, muscle fibers tear. These tears leave an empty space between the two "broken" ends of the fiber. Tiny, and sometimes, painful, these tears **do** repair. The blood running through your muscle tissue leaves behind small particles that fill the empty space, in turn becoming new muscle fiber. This expansion of the muscle fibers causes the muscle itself to become larger, or greater. Becoming larger, or greater, would be considered growth. So what's next? It's elementary. Stretch your mind. Yes, stretching your mind will create some *empty space* at times, but the tenure of the empty space is only momentary. The mind, like muscles, does have *blood flow*. It is the natural, innate process called thinking. Thinking produces thoughts, ideas, revelations, realizations, etc. These bi-products of thinking fill the empty spaces and, in return, the mind grows. As simple as it seems, stretching is viewed as being awkward and uncomfortable. Not in the dark. Catch on. Can't nobody see you in the dark. In the dark, the mind is unseen, giving it the freedom to have individuality, without scrutiny or social recourse. In defense to light, there is the possibility of stretching out and *bumping* into something, or someone, else unseen while in the dark. Stretch some more. It is called preparing for the unexpected. Whatever you bumped into will move around. Again, in defense to light, light is needed. Light is the preparation for the dark. Light is the zone of comfort where you can go to catch your breath. Light is the deep breath that is taken right before .... Light is the battle .... Dark is the war.

Peek-A-Boo Street

A person you may know;
One you may know not.
There's something about this one—
A person you have to got.

A person who sees face,
Intrigued by what they see.
Boredom of beauty comes,
Person *sets* the face "free."

Providers come with intent.
Person welcomes with a smile.
Providers' *resources* will get spent.
Person disappears after it's worth the while.

Person loves playing the game
Until they think there's no more to score.
For the other, their pride feels walked on
More than a living room floor.

Some personas you'll wanna burn.
Some personas you'll wanna meet.
Avoid the risk of wasting a turn—
Steer clear of Peek-A-Boo Street.

See Saw

There were many, many a day
Where we knew neither yea nor nay.
You *saw* our burdens as your own.
God gave you the perfect word to say.

When times were going well
It was as if you already knew.
You knew from spiritual confidence.
It was your prayers that *saw* me through.

Passing through tough times,
Seemingly driving all alone.
Beyond your words, I *saw* you
Holding my hand through the phone.

In times of confusion,
Indecisiveness in the air
I *saw* you tired and weary
From bellowing your caring prayer.

You *saw* the things that bothered me—
Things that warmed the ground under my feet.
I *see* you waving your colorful scarves.
From them, the breeze cools the heat.

While the world looks with a scowl,
Frowning the right into wrong,
I *see* your warm smile
While you sing your lovely song.

You epitomized being steadfast
You said "Give praise in **all** that you do."
Though I give praise for God's "calling,"
I still *see* you praising in the pew.

The things that I once *saw* you do,
I can't *see* them anymore.
But the things I *see* you doing now,
One day, I shall *see* plenty more.

Celebrating the Home Going

Of

Carlotta Eileen Harris Farris

Sunrise: February 7, 1949   Sunset: September, 7 2006

Say Word

Word—a brief remark or a written representation thereof; speech sound or series of speech sounds that communicate a meaning. Words—my ultimate source of pleasure. I am a lover of words. From short words like "a" and "I" to long words like "onomatopoeia," every word has a place and purpose in the world of self-expression. Words are never-changing while people are ever-changing. Words aren't manipulative or deceitful. Words aren't truthful or honest. Words are what people make them to be. Who a person really is can be seen through the words they use and by the way the use them. When words are used correctly, there is nothing else to be in need of. There is no need for anything other than what your body produces naturally (hold this thought). The right combination of words, themselves, is enough needed for one to accurately express themselves. The love comes from the combinations made from the words I use and who I am. (Release that thought) Tone of voice, body movements, gestures, and facial expressions: they all aid in the arousal of words. Words and people go hand-in-hand. People can't fully express themselves without using words and the beauty of any particular word cannot be fully portrayed without people using them. In my efforts of pure self-expression, words have never failed me. Words have never betrayed or forsaken me. Words have never let me down. Uncannily, words have always been aware of my mind's wit and clever "touch," yet they remained genuinely open to my interactions with them, knowing that I only intend to love them and treat them with the utmost dignity and respect. And they have treated me the same in return.

Not only am I a lover of words, I am a lover **to** words. There are many words that I know. There are even more words that I have no idea of their existence. Some words, I may have a slight understanding of their meanings. And then there are those words, regardless of whether I have seen or heard it before, or not, I know **exactly** what it means when I do *meet* it. Regardless of the extent of my knowledge of a particular word, I eventually become its lover after we meet. I take my time getting to know a word, learning its every intention and every possible direction for movement. I massage the word's temples. I rub the soles of its feet. And I caress every inch of its existence that lies in between. I stare deeply into the eyes of a word and kiss upon its lips. Light, tender kisses are placed upon the word's arms, breasts, belly, thighs, and calves. In the midst of the kisses, I come to the realization that all the work needed in order to enjoy knowing the word to its fullest satisfaction has been done. The word is now, willingly, at the mercy of my mind and hands. But in being one's lover, one knows that along with work needed, there is work desired as well. Work needed is **never** enough. The work desired is more than mutual, and the word and I enter into *the congress of a crow*. Not all words are blessed with a lover endowed in knowing how to travel the road to its ultimate satisfaction. But my words are, and they show their gratitude by giving *the kiss that turns away*. Exiting the crow's nest, I become the word's *missionary*; on top of everything, controlling every use of the word in my expressions. Knowing I'm in charge, I take the *elephant's posture*. The word's face lies gently on a pillow while possessing a gentle smile. The stimulation from the smile's catalyst is too much to take lying down. The word takes a *second posture* and calls upon *the white tiger*. All understanding in every aspect of the word is being taken with such forceful confidence and care, the word gains confidence in the relationship and decides to place me in *the swing*, reaching for a *pair of tongs* due to the companionship being too hot to handle with mere hands alone. Like *cat and mice sharing a hole*, the word and I reach a union, despite all indifferences and in light of all commonalities. After spinning *Kama's wheel*, the connection has been *sewn*, like that of *sutra*; Sanskrit, if you will.

All etymology aside, the wordsmith's libido is even greater for a more in-depth knowledge of the word. To the word, lover-boy is what I will always be: mind, body, soul, and spirit. And with that, I give my word. Word—a promise.

Say What?!?!

Talk is cheap . . . and it seems like the majority of everybody has a lot of it. On top of that, in lieu of talk's cheapness, people are **still** "broke" because the cheap price lures them into buying more than they need. "Do what you say, **THEN** say what you do." That will make your words more believable when you do say them. A person claiming to be honest will not be seen as such if all they do is lie. But, even a liar can be trusted and expected to be exactly that, if that **is** what they do. What one says should not tell of who they are, but, in fact, it should **validate** who they are. It is said that actions speak louder than words. That **is** true and could be true to all, but not all are listening with the right "ears." Even though actions have a loud voice, what speaks loudest of all is silence. When one doesn't "talk," others will seek and find what they want to know about you through your everyday, genuine actions and lifestyle. Silence makes the loudest statements of all, regardless of what the statement is. Yet, again, not everyone is listening with the right "ears." Speaking of statements, people don't fully understand that, with manifest statements, there **will** also be latent and lurking statements. And this goes beyond talking with spoken or written words. Moreover than anything else, people try to "talk" through materials and possessions. People spend **more** than way too much time trying to tell of themselves through materialism and don't realize that they've lost all knowledge of who they are to themselves in the process. There are several rhetorical questions that should and need to be answered . . . . . .after the removal of materials and possessions, or after "mouths" have been silenced, if you will. If a person had not the ability to "speak," how would others see or perceive them?

How would they see or perceive themselves? Who would they be to others? Who would they be to themselves? If the answer to any of these questions is "I don't know," or if the answer does **not** tell of whom they truly are, then, obviously, there are some problems. And to that: Baby doll, grab your mop and bucket. It's time to clean up; and lil' daddy, big daddy, baby's daddy—whoever, whatever: I don't give a fuck. Grab your hard hat and your tools. There's some shit to fix. At times, actions do speak louder than words. However, there are times when saying, or not saying, certain words will speak louder than what **any** action would.

Long Winter

I've felt this before.

Actually, not too long ago.

No matter what the season

The effects fall like a cold, winter snow.

I'm hungry, and food, I have not.

For right now, only the cold does grow.

I'm thirsty, without a possible quench.

For my river is frozen. There is no flow.

My lungs burn from the sharp air.

The steam escapes with every blow.

I've felt this before.

But, now, I feel somewhat loco.

All is frozen to me and, to all, I am the same.

I really want, desire, and need my cup of hot cocoa.

Who's Feeling What?!

Every single day, I think of you.

But my nerves are bothered because I'm with some other.

I'm tired from my efforts to find joy in them.

My heart is weary; my love for you I cannot completely smother.

You feel it because this is you to me, not me to you.

I try to be Gapetto, to pinnochio puppets in time,

But us being together is the closest thing to destiny.

I try, but there's no avoiding my deep desire for you.

Nothing will ever replace the "time" that you vested in me.

You feel it. True feelings are exactly that: true.

Red-orange leaves on trees and snow: close, but not quite right.

I know there's "perfect" compatibility between you and I.

I focus my attention on others because the truth scares me so.

I admit, I look away from you solely in denial. I cannot lie.

You feel it: "I should do what I 'know' to do."

Fuck You

This all started with your player pimp dreamin'.
You generational asshole. How the fuck I come from your semen?!

So far, it's been 327 months I've been looking for a hero.
Last time I counted, your bitch ass has showed up for zero.

I'm done being humble and these words are quite late.
You will always be the lesser. I will always be the great.

You can point and brag all you want, but why do you even bother?
There will never be anything of you in me. **I'm** my fuckin' father.

Are you fuckin' serious, requesting to know my me?!
No. Fucking. Way. You don't even know "D."

Punk ass baby kangaroo. Why you peekin' out the pouch?
You stood up the wrong way. You should've stayed yo' ass on the couch.

I'll never have to say I'm back because I'm never fuckin' leavin'.
I don't see why God has decided to leave yo' ass fuckin' breathin'.

Scared for you and the outcome, I will probably never speak.
But before I drop the pencil, I have one last thing to leak:

Fuck you.

You, Too!

Dear Love,

Right now, you are the most repulsive thing that I can fathom; yet, you are a part of me that will never go away. You are that part of me that I wish I could change, but can't change and, unfortunately, am stuck with 'til my dying days. What you can do right now is take yourself, place it as the recipient of "Fuck You," and suck a dick. You can eat shit and sip on a glass of piss on the rocks . . . . bitch.

Love,

Derrick E. Sumral

Snake Eyes
(Seeing Double)

I've been nothing but true—doubled over,
And been nothing but wronged—troubled over.
Well, it's time for change—no stumble over.
So, move out the way, or get rumbled over.

I'mma double down on the teddy bear
And double up on the grizzly bear.
I think I'll muzzle down Papa Bear.
A full Black Pearl all will have to bear.

I'mma double down on the kiss ass
And double up on the kick ass.
I'mma double up on the jackass
And double down on the lick ass.

I'mma double up on the fuck you's
And double down on my trust you's.
I'mma little tired of these damn blues;
Tired of bullshit on my damn shoes.

I'mma double up on my bust you's

And double down on my touch you's.

The invites, I'mma havtah put a hush to;

An inevitable something that I must do.

I'mma double up on my bite

And double down on my bark.

There will always be a word to say,

But louder are actions from the heart.

BOOK III

An Epic Battle

CHAPTER 9

Hidden Treasures

Somebody's Somebody

Nobody—not anybody; a person of no influence **or** consequence. Anybody—any person or anyone. Somebody—one or some person of unspecified or indefinite identity; or, also, a person of position or importance. A nobody is just . . . there. Nothing more. Nothing less. Being a nobody . . . it's simple. Simply don't do **anything**. Anybody can be a nobody. But not just anybody can be a somebody. Do something . . . and you will be a somebody to somebody. Everybody—every person or everyone. Generally, everybody has at least one somebody. Typically, everybody is somebody to himself or herself. There's nothing wrong with that. Everybody should have a positive perception of himself or herself. Unfortunately, there is a portion of everybody whose only somebody **is** himself or herself. That's vain—useless and self-centered. It is pointless to be important to oneself and not share that importance with somebody else. A position of importance is best given when given by somebody else. One body feels more like a somebody when somebody else expresses the importance of that one body. However, the importance can't be one-sided. Console in somebody in good times as well as the bad times. Going to somebody only in bad times is called "dumping." Nobody wants to be dumped on. When somebody is dumped on, they sometimes feel like . . . a nobody. A somebody is one that will laugh with you, cry with you, and even be dry with you. Why? Well, usually, when somebody is a somebody to you, you are probably a somebody to that somebody as well. Some people need their position of importance expressed to them daily for them to know they are a somebody. Others can go years without their importance expressed to them; yet they know they are a somebody to somebody. It is all in how the importance is expressed. Some expressions are spoken words. Some expressions may come by way of actions. Regardless of how the importance is expressed, God made everybody a somebody: a somebody with discernment. Anybody can use their discernment to figure out the frequency and method of expression needed to express somebody's importance to that somebody. All it takes is for somebody to do something for somebody to feel like a somebody. So, regardless of how big or small the something is, somebody do something, because there isn't anybody who **wants** to feel like nobody...nobody.

Dedicated to my Brothers:

paternal ("G" and "Fatz"); kin ("Sixty"); friend ("Jab");

& My Nigga's (they know who they are)

To the Death

Till death do us part. That is how this arranged marriage shall end. A marriage arranged by my Father: he blessed Life with me, and he blessed me with Life. But a choice, he gave to neither of us. A choice that is a two-edged sword. The second edge ... if you don't want to choose Life, then ... I guess ... the only other choice is ... Death. Death ... I definitely choose not. The first edge ... Life ... a very unfaithful Life ... a cheater. Life fully understands the meaning of monogamous, but, unfortunately, will never practice it. Life is *involved* with every single being that will ever exist. The tenure of some *involvements* are longer than others, but no one goes without being involved with Life. Being an involved partner, or spouse, if you would, Life does bring smiles, laughter, sunshine, joy, and soft touches. However, being involved with so many different partners, it is nothing but inevitable for Life to be unfaithful. I can't, and won't, say that Life is unfaithful more than it is faithful. But when it cheats, it always seems to hit hard, seemingly erasing all that is good that it has done. Life is not the innocent cheat either. Life is that "bold, pompous, slap you in the face, kick you in the ass, and smile about it" cheat. And there is nothing, absolutely nothing, that you can do about it ... unleeeess ... naaaah, don't be stupid. The second edge is not an option, at least not *my* option. I'll just deal with it and let Life get away with it. Maybe, if I stay honest and faithful myself, Life might just see the "wrong" in "its" ways and grow a conscience. Then, in turn, it will be faithful to being faithful to me **all** the time .... fuuuuck **that**. One would be foolish and idiotically naïve to believe that Life would ever be faithful to **one** person. Life ... what to do with it? Orrrrrrrr, what to do with something else? That's it! I'll just be a cheater, myself.

When I think about it, I have actually been cheating on Life since I was eleven years old. At around 7 or 8 years old, when I really understood how to spell Words, I began to flirt with Words. I started going to word whorehouses and gentlemen's clubs (dictionaries and thesauruses). There, I would use my eyes to strip them naked, just to see what they had to offer. I tipped them occasionally, using them in a thought or sentence from time to time, but that was about it. Although, I had this uncanny desire to know them, I never saw a need for them beyond everyday conversation … until … the sixth grade. I was given a **homework** assignment to write a poem. I *thought* I needed Life's help, but Life was out foolin' around with someone else. For a split second, I truly felt alone. Then Words began to come to me. It was as if they remembered my gentle "touches" from times before. It wasn't but five minutes after the assignment was given that my first written poem was born. I was quite appreciative of the Words that came to me. So appreciative that I began to confide in them about everything: joy … sorrow … pleasure … pain … thoughts of reflection … thoughts of revelation. Initially, Words were just a mistress—I went to them at my convenience. But over time, the relationship between Words and I have become an unbreakable companionship, whether I get caught or not. Words are my release.

At some time, and I couldn't tell you when even if I wanted to, "touching" just wasn't enough anymore. When I shared time with Words, I only heard my voice: thinking and reading. But I continued in my affair with Words because Life was still in-and-out and Words were all I had. Then, again, comes an assignment forcing temptation upon me. This assignment required a prolonged tenure (2 semesters) of use of a vessel that aids in one's musical expression. The only vessels I had were a pencil, a pad, and my voice. While walking through a hall built for musical curriculum, contemplating my options … I heard her. Pianessa. She spoke to me like a silky whisper from sweet lips floating on the waves of the wind's ocean. With no consultation between my spirit and soul, my entire being was anxious to intertwine our worlds. In the beginning stages of our relationship, I didn't apply myself like I wanted to. I didn't have the time to. My neglect to her began to grow, and in correlation, so did my woes within. A crowd of years had passed when, one day, I simply looked at her and she called my name. I went to her, sat down, and caressed her body with my fingers. I began to play as if I had never left her side. It was as if she **understood** why I hadn't touched her in so long. I don't think she agreed, but who was I to complain. I couldn't, and I wouldn't, for she was, and is, my sound. When Life was not there, and I didn't feel like hearing the words of myself, I could listen to the voice that I gave to Pianessa. Her lullaby is my therapy.

In life, there has been, are, and will be many a people who will say something like this: "I am never going to be like that," or "I am never going to be like him/her." Ironically, most of them try so hard to avoid being a certain way, something, or somebody, that their focus has them seeing only what they don't want to be, blinding them from their alternative, hence becoming exactly what they didn't want to become because that is all they allowed themselves to see. As much as I despise Life for its unfaithfulness, I've become exactly like it. The longer I cheat, the more I want to. And the more I cheat, the longer I want to. I've become greedy... just like Life. But Life was **still** one-up on me. Life is unfaithful just because it can be. For me, Words and Pianessa came about from necessity. I could have chosen not to partake in our interactions; however, I would have faced setbacks within the social institution of education. I needed a conquest that I **wanted**... just for the fuck of it. And I've had my eye on her for quite some time. Enter stage right: Evelynn Acoustica. She has the neck of a graceful gazelle, a perfectly curvaceous body that molds to my lap as if she was meant to be there all along, and a voice with versatility that can make anyone move, given the time to. She being a mistress of mine is perfect: she brings comfort like that of Words and she speaks the same language as Pianessa. But, yet, she is still one in her own. Words are **always** there, even when I'm with Pianessa and Evelynn. But, sometimes, I can't be "seen" with Words in public. Words have to come out at the right time in some occasions.

Pianessa, as beautiful as she is, I can't take her everywhere I want to. She is a homebody. She does have "cousins" that I play with as well, but they, too, would rather stay in the comfort of home, for the most part. But Evelynn . . . she can be butt naked and still be more than ready to hop on my back and face the world. She wants to be next to me. Her total being is, and will be, my sidekick.

On our separate paths to complete companionship, I have noticed that Life and I, both, have made attempts to make amends to each other. I have tried to face Life as a man and tell it about my mistresses, but just as the time becomes right, Life runs off to one of its "others." On many occasions, Life has tried to pleasure me with a being comparable and compatible to myself. I've watched Life do the same for others when it wants to be unfaithful to them as well. In that, Life is no respecter of men. Sometimes, those pleasures are satisfactory. Sometimes, it takes sifting through several options of pleasure for one to be satisfied. For me, the pleasures come and go. Some, I'd rather them go, and, some, I'd rather they stay. But for now . . . I have my mistresses. Words . . . well, they are my words. Pianessa is my language. And Evelynn . . . she is the accent. All together, they are like hearing the native tongue from the lips of a beautiful Latin woman. Regardless of if Life brings to me my ultimate pleasure, my mistresses will be with me to the death . . . including Life.

Have You Ever...

Have you ever...

Had someone touch your skin so well

That your body will always carry their pleasant smell?

Have you ever...

Had someone whose beauty was not of men,

Whose hair moved as if it were silk in the wind?

Have you ever...

Had someone kiss your jaw

And it felt like you were touched by a kitten's paw?

Have you ever...

Had someone with perfect hips,

Ample breasts, gorgeous eyes, and luscious lips?

Have you ever...

Had someone hold you in their grasp,

Staring at the stars, hoping the time would forever last?

Have you ever…

Had someone and loved their name,

And thought of their cuddling every time it rained?

Have you ever…

Had someone rest the head on your shoulder

And you felt as one, neither being younger or older?

Have you ever…

Had someone speak to your spirit

And their voice drifts you away every time you hear it?

Have you ever…

Had someone in whom there was a destined love

Because you knew they were an angel sent from above?

Have you ever…

Had someone in whom you could kiss & tell

And no matter what is said, you know all would be well.

Have you ever…

Had someone, even for just a day or two,

That no matter what happened, their love would always stay with you?

Have you ever…

Had someone so honest and true

That they meant every word in saying their someone is you?

Half Full Half Empty

Is the glass half full? Or, is the glass half empty? Asking me of my view, in all due respect to yourself, don't tempt me. Intertwining one living by the spirit of faith with one living unfaithful in whole; they both share one soul. Like that of a magnet, the north and south both share a central pole. A heart full of passion, burning wildly, a driving desire grows. La corazon de frio con cold-hearted veins pumped with ice water colder than a thousand snows. Both share in being one heart. From them both, a source of life flows. The optimist smiles, finds comfort, and can unconsciously become complacent. The pessimist snarls, often standing stagnant, making turns quite adjacent. The optimist glances back, sees the pessimist and doesn't want to fall behind. The pessimist looks ahead, seeing the optimist in the light, wanting his own piece of the sun's shine. Between the two, the other needs the other. They motivate each other. Their polaric pushes keep their balance aligned. But the pessimist and the optimist, I pay attention to neither of the two. There is a greater perspective shared between them; in paying attention to, neither of them do. You can put aside the debate and do away with the society's wrath. A glass half full or a glass half empty: either way . . . . you only have **one** half. Is the glass half full? Or, is the glass half empty? Asking me of my view, in all due respect to yourself, don't tempt me . . . . get your other half.

Simple Song . . .

Childhood desires within a childhood crush. Genuine. Authentic.

Friendship full of happiness, not caring if the milkman drops a glass bottle.

Even then, the spill is not the focus. Cleaning up the spill is.

Understanding. Not necessarily agreeing, but understanding.

Compromises and sacrifices lead to mutual assurances.

Beauty shining from within throughout. And they see you the same way.

What a simple and wholesome song to sing.

. . . Complex Melody

Childhood doesn't last forever . . . you grow. Polished. Distinguished.

Experiences, happy and sad, alter perspectives. Wisdom gained.

Life is not all gloom. It only seems easier to see it that way.

A Black Gospel song. A few sharps. Several flats and minor chords.

To some, a difficult style to learn, but, to more, a beautiful song to hear.

Turning **everything** into a positive, even if it is already there.

What a complex, but beautiful and satisfying, melody to follow.

I Forgot To Remember

It sometimes seems as though no matter what I do, it is never good enough. Never good enough for whomever, and at times, even myself. And let's say what I do **is** satisfactory. Then the way I did it is not. Missed opportunities, bad timings, wrong decisions, unwise choices . . . all ways in which I have fallen. But every time, I've gotten up. Maybe not standing as tall as before, but, I've gotten up; however . . .

. . . I forgot to remember . . . Falling down is not necessarily failure; yet, it is an opportunity to rise, and rise standing stronger and taller than before. Never remember to forget falling. Remember the fall, but don't dwell on it. Try to grow from it. Forgetting a fall only invites the same fall to re-occur. Regardless of who or what caused you to fall, never forget to remember . . .

Hidden Treasures

Sometimes, people come across things that they honestly didn't mean to and/or expect to. Karma has its way of showing its sense of "humor" by "protecting" things that may be misplaced or lost-protected as in letting them stay lost until their original owner finds them or they are turned in to appropriate personal for a rightful claiming and lost as in they weren't meant to be found by someone else. In fact, they weren't meant to be lost in the first place. And, when found, these things are often seen as treasures—treasure as in it has some sense of value to its owner, or any other person obtaining possession of it, for that matter. Majority of the time, when what is lost becomes found, the finder usually knows that it has been lost, as goes the same for what has been hidden. Hidden treasures, when found, are usually known as having been hidden. There's just something about them that says "hidden." Usually, where and how it was found suggests that it was purposely placed there. Losing a treasure is generally accidental, where; on the other hand, hiding one is intentional. It only makes sense to intentionally hide something that is of value, or treasured. The "value" of the treasure to its owner may be so high that the owner would like to the treasure it entirely for himself … or *to* himself. Or the value of the treasure may me so low that the owner would not want anyone else to know of its existence. Regardless of whether the treasure is lost, hidden, proudly valued, or shamefully possessed, the thing about treasures is they are usually and eventually found … or found out about … by someone other than the hiding owner. The perception of the treasure is highly influenced by whether the treasure was lost or hidden and by why the treasure is so highly, or lowly, valued. The correlation of the two is what causes the treasure to have an impact on one's life. Not only does the perception of the treasure impact the life of its owner, but when the treasure ends up in the hands of another, **that** person will more than likely form the same perception of the treasure and their life will be impacted as well. With the way the world is, perception seems to be everything. With that said, is a treasure really a treasure if it is shamefully hidden? Wouldn't it be safer to avoid the detriment of said treasures by disassociating oneself from the treasure entirely? But some treasures have been "clung" on to for so long that a disassociation would not be simple ... or easy ... or, even possible. Treasures should be chosen wisely: a treasure can build one up, or break one down. Be careful in what you treasure, for even when you are "gone," **it** will become found ... exactly the same way you "hid" it.

Eternal Lifelong
Eternity

Doubtful to ever forget,

    memories that all souls long for and desire to cherish.

Every soul has potential mates,

    but the pairing of these two make even the happy jealous.

Lushingly and oh-so lovingly,

    it brings a flavor to life that the soul will relish.

Every moment is precious,

    the desire for a blending of auras is simply sweetly zealous.

Eye for beauty has the heart,

    passionate in finding life, a life to embellish

Symbolic of all that is forever,

    throughout triumphs **and** trials, it will never perish … it is …

Eternal.

Delightful is the upcoming present,

    A satisfying and edifying life full of glee.

Every day will be **the** day;

    as long as every day is spent with thee.

Love, in its purest form,

    is blissful, and days of bliss will forever be.

Eternity has blinded my eyes,

> the end of an undying love, I will never see.

Even death has no say,

> the spirit will forever stay. It will never flee.

Silent it may become,

> But it will never stop loving from a bended knee …

Everlasting … Lifelong.

Divine intervention—no coincidence;

> supernatural favor is the only explanation.

Ever-so precisely created,

> a relationship meant for total, complete jubilation.

Loose with laughter, yet tight with input:

> a gem of sweet-hearted saturation.

Enticed by appeal, engulfed in authenticity;

> a treasure of love **and** infatuation.

Earnest in needs and desires,

> an intertwining union yearning for maturation.

Sands of time will never stop:

> an everlasting journey caught in sweet captivation … of …

Eternity.

Your Hands

I miss your hands across my back, while standing chin to chin.
I miss your hands fairing me well and welcoming me back in.

I miss your hands always lifting me up when I stumble.
I miss your hands restraining me ego, keeping the proud humble.

I miss your hands brushing my face, cradled across my cheek.
I miss your hands pulling me near, allowing our souls to speak.

I miss your hands covering my mouth when my words are too loud.
I miss your hands sitting me down when my walk would get too proud.

I miss your hands inspecting every inch of my fade.
I miss your hands showing appreciation for every new *time* made.

I miss your hands' clap, uplifting, even when my own claps were few.
I miss your hands' vision, always finding a way to see things through.

I miss your hands warmth, open-palmed, resting on my chest.
I miss your hands safe assurance, cuddled with mine, tucked below your breast.

My hands miss holding your hands; through them we speak without sound.

My life misses the hold of your hands; in them is where my true joy is found.

I miss your hands' kiss at the dawn's calling on me to wake.
I miss your hands' song, lullabying me 'til the next day to break.

I miss your hands' discovery, finding the man that sleeps within.
I miss your hands' company, company found only in a best friend.

I miss your hands' direction, sharing pathways to greater bliss.
In all of the ways they have touched me, your hands I sure do miss.

Ariel

…you arrived unexpectedly
the very thought of you was nothing less than wonder
your presence was serene like rain with no thunder
the joy you personalized, no one can possibly plunder

for truth in the word, you brought love's purity
for everything good in life, you brought surety
in regards to your own, life gave no security
you departed unexpectedly…

When the Shoe Fits . . .

There are things in life that just seem to fit. Regardless of the angle of approach, they just fit. Upon my first entrance into the Slitheran House, literally and figuratively, I recognized some familiar "faces" from childhood and there were some faces that were relatively new. Being an introvert, what I felt, however, was totally unrecognized. Before the entrance, my *brother*, Sixty the Great, had mentally prepared me for the atmosphere and comradery, but (a **BIG** but), I had to see it for myself. Sixty introduced to all those that were present. In light of the host/guest relationship, there was the customary introductory dap and "what's ups," but I was watching them ... and they were watching me. But why? Over the numerous months and visits that followed, I watched. And I observed. And every time I left, when I left, I felt as if someone had been thumbing through my pages, trying to read me. One night in particular, it fell into place for me.

Everything that I had felt and observed began to piece together like a 20-something piece puzzle. In the midst of music playing and passing conversations, not even being a part of The House yet, I wrote what has been called The House "Anthem". The purpose of the "anthem" was simply to be a written account of my observations of several differences, experiences, skills, knowledge, abilities, and intellects within the House individuals meshed together to make a single, solid unit. I have never been one to "pledge my allegiance" to any "crew" or circle of friendship. I've always been a solo artist with a select few of close friends, holding my own ... me taking care of me. But with The House, there was no feeling of being a crutch: only there to lean on you when everyday movement is hindered. There are no single, brightest stars. Only brightly shining stars, shining together to make a galaxy. It was a comradery that fit to my liking. And, evidently, I fit to their liking because they invited me in. Upon the invitation, there is a meeting to obtain a House census: a time for those presently in The House to discuss the pros and cons of inviting another in. The invitation is sealed when the newly invited has consumed a considerable amount of liquor via numerous shots. At first thought, I just thought it was a ritual. At about my seventh or eighth shot of Pearl Vodka and third or fourth cup of the "sauce," I realized that the consumption was secondary. The primary was entrusting my well-being within a group of guys, and a girl (What up, Paparazzi?!), and not worrying about if they would take care of me, but actually knowing that they would. Sixty: I had no doubts. But what if Sixty wasn't there? **That** question lasted a total of three seconds, if that long. Partly because I was highly intoxicated and my shortened attention span would not allow me to entertain the thought long enough to think of an answer. And partly because I felt I could trust them. The relationship was cemented with the passing of two messages. One, I can trust you (them): through thick and thin. And, two, you can trust me: through thick and thin. Both shoes were the same size, and they fit. Now in the midst of the consumption of the shots, the consumer will be watched and observed by The House, and a House nickname will be given to them based on what they do while you are "lost". A lot of the time, when I talk (verbal or written), I become a little long-winded. I like for my listener to have as many details as possible. Well, just imagine that compounded with being "lost." Needless to say, my House name is N.E.S. Never-Ending Story. The name is quite fitting . . . in more ways than one. My book—Since it is about my life, it will never end . . . until I die. And even then, it shall never end. At her early age, I am instilling in my daughter my writing ways so that when Daddy is gone, she can continue the book with writings of her own. Females—A lot times, the relationships I have with females become never-ending stories. I do what I do . . . and I do it well. My Voyage of Cultivation—it is a never-ending story. I will never cease to cultivate myself as a human being . . . person . . . man . . . . when the shoe fits . . . I wear it.

Derrick E. Sumral, a.k.a. N.E.S.

The Day We First Met

It's as if your eyes whispered to my heart
And your lips kissed my soul.
Your smile grabbed my hand
And made me whole.

Truth be told …
Before I me   ou …
I longed to hold you.
Now that I have you …
I thank GOD for you!
With this blessing I shall never regret.
For I cherish the eighteenth of May; the day we first met.

Zena Levine

June 6, 2007

Charm School

It is said that you learn something new every day.

Then that would make living life an everyday school.

If the saying, "the more you know, the more you grow" is true,

Then, to not know, when you could, would be worse than being a fool.

There are some that hit the books all day: professional students.

And others that hit the streets all day: school of hard knocks.

From my earliest recollection, **I** live in the school of thought,

But my school of choice is the one where the foxtails trot.

There are no grades to earn for efforts put forth,

For there is not a curriculum for a student to follow.

Credit is earned from an entrapment of the graders:

Sensuality lasting through tomorrow's tomorrow.

My "Piece"

I was reading my Bible … yes, my Bible. I think reading it is vital for my survival. And if you are now angry, uneasy, or squirmin' … you **can** keep reading. This is not a conviction. This is not a sermon. Basically, I came across a passage, and my thoughts would not let me pass it.

"Never let loyalty (love) and kindness (faithfulness) get away from you! Wear them like a necklace; write them deep in your heart."

Proverbs 3:3, NLT (New Living Translation)

The part of the scripture that grabbed my attention was "Wear them like a necklace …" For the most part, a necklace is an article of declaration. There is a degree of attention that is desired to be obtained through the necklace, meaning the wearer wants the necklace to be seen. And, to assure attention is obtained, the necklace is sometimes accompanied by a charm, or, also called, a piece. When worn, this piece becomes the primary focal point and the necklace itself becomes secondary. The piece makes a more specific statement than the necklace. It usually symbolizes something that bears significance to the wearer. I, personally, have three necklaces that I wear consistently. Ironically, all three of them bear the same piece: the letter "D." "D" is me and I am "D." That "letter" and I will forever have an unexplainable bond and anyone who bestows upon any of my necklaces can safely assume that "D" and I are one in the same. Two of my three necklaces are necklaces that I can physically put on and take off at my discretion. The third necklace and its "D," its "piece," is one that **cannot** be taken off. Also, it **cannot**, and **will not**, go unnoticed. Ironically, the necklace that cannot be tangibly touched is the one that is most visible. Visible beyond the plain sight of the naked eye, but most visible to the eyes of the heart. This necklace is who I am. Not Derrick, the person, but Derrick, the man. This necklace is my personality. My sense of humor. My temperament. My outspokenness. My eminence. My distinction. This necklace is my character. My confidence. My humility. My honesty. My trust. My loyalty. My faith. My love. My hatred. All of these things of me, and much more, are my inner man, and I "wear them like a necklace": a necklace that **cannot** be purchased . . . by anyone. It can only be fabricated and that fabrication can only exist through the forging of time (experiences); however, myself, and others, can influence its purity. But, ultimately, **I** am the jeweler. I am also the crafter of its piece. A piece worthy of grand scale size and luster due to the extravagance of its necklace, but a piece that is simply my satisfaction in wearing the necklace itself. This piece is my pride in being me. This piece is my peace.

Fire, Flame, Friction

Slyhouse is The Fire, burning with immense and intense heat. Not a wildfire spreading out of control, foolishly consuming everything in its path by way of destruction, but a controlled and strategically set fire, with a widespread consumption of intrigue and excitement by way of a multi-faceted expression of mental and artistic exploration, entertaining the masses, large and small, with a foremost intent of heightening the "heat" of **each** of The Fire's individual Flames.

Those within Slyhouse are The Flames, each with their own individual source of "heat," but neither with the intent to burn hotter or brighter than any of the other flames, yet sacrificial with their heat, giving of themselves, in attempt to keep all individual flames burning. Not to say a flame's heat cannot reach a higher degree, but when it does, the heat is applied to The Fire. Though they may be similar, no Flame is identical in its source of heat, giving The Fire multiple and diverse avenues in which to burn. There can be neither a fire without flames … nor a flame without a spark … … a spark induced by friction.

Within each Flame, there is friction, an abrasive rubbing between the will to, not only survive, but excel, and the elements of life that pose as opposition. These elements consist of more than those of triteness—racial, economical, geographical, and gender barriers. There are intra-personal elements as well—illiteracy, stagnancy, self-discipline, and the lack thereof. These elements create a transparent box of premature satisfaction and complacency, surrounding all that allow themselves to succumb to its very presence. This box is non-existent as a unit of containment to the

Sly; yet, it is our foundation, and on top of it we stand firm. Our feet tread heavily and forcefully atop of this box. The friction of our steps creates the sparks that fuels The Fire. These sparks (i.e., movements and endeavors) are seen by all, some of who desire these sparks to be of their own. They are not, and metamorphically those desires become intrigue and excitement, in which The Fire consumes.

We are not an affiliation, association, committee, or brotherhood. We are a family of families and comradery, well beyond any titles of grouping given by man.

We are Slitheran.

N.E.S.

Blurry Vision

Alarm clock sounds. Still tired. On my knees while I sleep.
Today I will feel like Jesus when he's holding the baby *sheep*.

I dress neat and comfortable, preparing for the ride.
And inside, my pride can't hide, for it is beaming through my
hide.

The voices of the day, they all sound like worthless chatter.
The gas prices of the day, they don't even seem to matter.

Driving along and can't see a thing, so think is all I do.
Everything just seems so blurry, but I **always** see Exit 222.

I know it is coming and it is exactly what I need:
A lunging, leaping hug, launched from a running that is
full-speed.

Enjoying my turns like that of a top's fuzzy spins,
I want to **really** enjoy this. Can the view clear up before it ends?

With laughs to still laugh, hugs to still give, and other things to
do,

Everything on this ride is really blurry now. I wish there was no
Exit 222.

Our traditional game of I-Spy and "I'm gonna miss you" make me
realize
That the cause of my blurry vision is the built-up tears in *our*
eyes.

Chapter 10

Re-Masted

The New YOUth

They give ... but can't, won't, and don't give.

They are bright ... but not very bright.

They are smart ... but refuse to be smart.

They have life ... but don't know how to live.

They can see ... but are blinded by sight.

They are proud ... but have no sense of pride.

They are mighty ... but are wounded by might.

They have tried ... but have not tried.

They are quite ... but they are just not quite ...

Change

I am change;

a refreshing and needed change for humanity's future.

They see change;

offering handshakes, pats-on-the-back, and kudos for the good that is to come.

They, too, see change;

yearning for personal growth . . . dejected because handshakes and etc. are quite limited to them.

I change;

now, myself, needing to be refreshed in order to **face** humanity's future.

They haven't changed;

still handing out praises, only because they see the change **they** need to be, but can't be.

They don't change:

from seeing Change change due to a lack of change, they are deterred.

Gone Camping

Where am I? Going *left* was a *wrong* turn.

Taking heed to my directions I truly must learn.

I don't want to be camping …

I need a hat. It is extremely cold.

Socks for gloves and drawers on my head have become extremely old.

This is the wrong season to be camping …

Thieves, murderers, rapists, dope heads, … a tramp;

These ain't the same kids from Summer Camp.

There are some interesting characters camping …

These grounds of recreation are not my choice,

And to them, casted away due to the words that others voice.

They sent me camping … and for what?

Achy Knees

For a long time, I carried a light weight, back when I thought I was completely strong.

I thought I had the will power to control **any**thing . . . and I was completely wrong.

For years, I ignored the pain I suffered from the burden that mounted heavier all the long.

Legs nearly crushed and a back hunched over; too out of breath to continue singing life's song:

Somebody, **PLEASE**, take this weight off my achy knees!

Forced to the ground was I, and there I felt quite comfortable and content to stay.

There, my tears soaked the ground at which I knelt; my tears being the least of prices I should pay.

Intense in fashion, kneeling I will stay; my sacred utterances causing clouds of gray.

For myself and others, I will kneel, interceding for the shouldered burdens of our day-to-day:

Lord, **please**, hear the cries I weep from my achy knees . . .

Forever I will kneel and bow to you, for I know you will always be forever there.

I will treat the under-knelt before me as an altar, where you are always just and fair.

And my then knelt altar shall be lifted, lovingly floating in the air;

For I'll be resting in your palms, where weight, neither shoulder nor knee will, no longer have to bear:

Father, please, accept my thanks for relieving my achy knees.

Goodbye, and Hello

My Dear Lady,   December 4, 2010

It has been over half a decade since I last wrote to you. I remember telling you to Breathe ... and the time is now for **me** to do the same, for I have been holding my breath since then. Holding my breath in wait of your arrival ... in wait of your recognition ... in wait of your acceptance ... neither of which ever came. I kept visions of you in my thoughts and held your warm embrace captive within my heart ... neither of which materialized. I became weak and my desire for you became faint, until **I** fainted ... and, then, was revived. Everything that I ever needed and desired had come and held me in her arms as I remained unconscious in an emotional coma. She touched me with hands of nurture, reaching beyond my outer surface and massaging my inner man. She spoke to me with a voice of sincerity, echoing her message of pure and genuine admiration throughout my entire being. She kissed me with lips of patience, wrapping her tongue around my heart and melting away the rock-hard ice that had forever engulfed it. She loved me, selflessly submerging her life into mine, giving me life anew. But even in the greatness of that, **I** almost lost **her** ... for when I came to; I treated her as if she were you. And **you**? **You**, all along, were just a desired craving of my lustful flesh ... a mere figment of my carnal imagination. In holding my breath, I had self-inflicted an emotional suffocation in wait of nothing; and to ensure that I do not put to death my life anew, my dear lady, I must breathe one last breath to you in the form of "Goodbye" ... and Hello, my dear Zena ...

I don't know what else to say,

Derrick

Epiphany

My Dear Lord,

There have been three young ladies that I have shed tears for in my life. Three different journeys . . . one common destination. And neither of the three offered even the least of a tissue to *truly* dry my eyes. Not to say that I was a perfect man, because I wasn't; but I transgressed not to deserve the heartbreaks that I received. And knowingly so, you were Always There. And upon crying to you, you would not allow the such. Your hands were not seen, but they dried my eyes. Upon seconds of the first drop, my tears you ceased from falling. Why not let me weep at **your** feet, Father? . . . There was no need to, for you had given me reason not to **well** before my first outpour. And it will be for that very same reason that my next tears shed for **any** female will be when I next wrap my arms around my daughter. **She** is my love. **She** is my pride. **She** is my joy. When I look upon her, I see the love of my brother, Jesus: pure, authentic, genuine, and unconditional. That is the way she has **always** loved me and that is the way I will **always** love her . . . forevermore. **She** is My Dear Lady. Without **her**, my heart would have stopped beating a long time ago. I thank you for your loving kindness in blessing me with her. Amen.

Your son,

Derrick

Iscariot

I know a man. A man, who, himself, knows right from wrong; good from evil. A man who dwells among those who are, and desires to be, righteous; however, he is sometimes led astray by certain enticements of evil.

This man has a friend. A friend who, in all his ways, strived to be moral and upright. This man loved his friend. He followed the ways of his friend. He took care of his friend. He sponsored his friend. He supported his friend. He defended his friend. Yet, when the opportunity for personal gain presented itself, the man befriended his friend. He went as far as betraying his friend to obtain the personal gain. The man was offered a purse to expose his friend, and he did. The man took the first thirty years of his friend's life and sold them, each for a silver coin apiece. The friend was taken away and persecuted for accusations placed against him. The persecution of the friend seemed to be the death of him; yet, it was the exact opposite. The persecution did not kill the friend, yet it conversely made the friend stronger than what he was before the persecution; giving him a life anew. Meanwhile, the man, overwhelmed by the guilt of his transgression, attempted to take his own life by hanging himself from a tree. Being that the man was not *skilled* at *knot tying*, his noose gave way and the man fell lifeless to the ground.

In passing, the friend crossed the man lying on the ground, raises the man to his feet, and reconciled their friendship unconditionally. It would have been unfortunate it not so. The actual death of either of the two would have been catastrophic. The death of one would have been the death of the other: the man and the friend were one in the same. I am that man … I am that friend … I was my own Judas of Iscariot.

While Amongst the Lost . . .

In being a person, I felt my most discomfort while gathered amongst the lost. The roads, of each one, journeyed: some parallel in nature, some perpendicular, others adjacent, and some of a tangent; most of which had not a visible destination. My journey was one of tangent. In the middle of my road, I stopped and stood still. I turned and observed the others. Those that were traveling in parallel fashion were now either perpendicular or adjacent of each other; the once perpendicular and adjacent were hence parallel. Why the change in the directions of their paths? They were blindly bouncing about off each other's journeys. Mass confusion was the order, with order being a concept that will never breed of an existence. All of those moving along their roads were lost. Some journeyed freely while others showed obvious signs of frustration; all of whom journeyed as if they *had* to travel in their current direction: ever-changing current directions ceased by the zigzag redirections from trying to conform to the roads taken by the others lost. The spontaneous and sporadic redirection of their journeys preoccupied their inner beings so much that a sense of purpose would never be fathomed . . . not even at the least . . .

... *I Realized* ...

In my state of idle observation, I was mentally, emotionally, physically, and spiritually able to *see* beyond those of whom I was gathered and I saw the *rest* of the general society. What I *saw* outside the confinement of the gathered was no different than what I saw within the gathered: misconception, deception, confusion ... lost souls. The only difference I saw was the gathered's absence of *freedom* to roam blindly outside the walls of confinement.

I, also, observed that there were others, like myself, whose journeys were of complete tangents, but most of who *moved* only to avoid the souls of the lost; taking them off their straight paths and causing them to be momentarily lost, themselves. I, myself, did not want to journey as if I were one of the lost; neither did I want to journey as if I were unaware of the lost's obliviousness of being lost. It wasn't until **my** path was crossed that I caught a glimpse of my own destination; with my destination being not that of a specific location, but that of a specific purpose. When my path was crossed, the **lost** stopped moving, causing them to realize for themselves that they were lost **and** understanding they didn't *have* to be lost. Internally, my purpose was realized. I was not to stand still, but to be in motion; being ready to cause a momentary pause of realization in the *paths* of others I may cross.

... *I Found Myself*

The Compass

At times, one may become lost in the midst of a journey and frustration may set in; especially if the journey is not one of their own. It is in these times when a source of guidance is greatly appreciated. The purpose of The Compass is to point the mind in a direction of familiarity and/or relativity. The Compass is not a full explanation of *The Voyage*; yet, it is simply a basic and foundational elucidation on which the mind may gather its "steps" and continue along the journey whenever redirection is needed.

Book I—The Preparation

A collection of training-like "battles" before traveling to war...

Chapter 1—The Beginning

As early as grade school, I always had rhyming phrases running through my mind. But, it wasn't until the 6th grade that I actually put the words on paper. The English *homework* assignment was to write a short poem. Five minutes after the assignment was given, **The Mac** was written...

The Mac—It tells of how being the lil' guy in school left you girl-less...

My Moms—I refer to my mother in plural. I don't know why... I just do. And this poem describes how I viewed my mother ... and still do ... (I wrote this poem as the actual homework assignment.)

Chapter 2—Itchy Finger

Itchy Finger refers to the point in time when one is ready to "pull the trigger" and just **one** more thing is all it is going to take for you to do so ...

What You Are—Sophomore year in high school; a particular girl whom I was writing letters to questioned my feelings for her. This poem was my response ...

What I Like—I was becoming annoyed by a certain "peoples" *concern* about who I chose to be interested in ...

If I Could—My general feelings before I finally decided to make my move(s) ...

The Scar—I cut open my upper lip on a broken locker. I later found out that some guy set up the accident while my back was turned, thinking it would be funny ...

To Have You—More general feelings before I finally decided to make my move(s) ...

What Is It?—I would try to figure out what attracted me to particular girls before I approached them ...

The Unknown—Mixed signals from a particular girl had me a little confused ...

The Kiss—Those mixed feelings were just a smoke screen…

Un-Touchable, Believable, Forgotten?—An ex-girlfriend and I decided to be a couple again…

Swings—Upholding a spiritual lifestyle can have its challenges…

What Can I Do?—Sometimes, the attraction is just that strong…

Versus—Two girls…unknowingly, wanting the same guy… who wins?

Stage Fright—High School Graduation…

Chapter 3—The Calm Before the Storm

Before every storm, there is an eerie, somewhat deathly, calmness in the air…

Neither a Beginning, Nor an End—When love comes about, you seldom know when it truly began … or how far it will go…

¿Love?—I had always had a particular "fascination" with a particular *woman*. This poem solidifies the fascination. Who is this *woman*? (Pay close attention to the title.)

Everlasting—Pre-marital emotions…

Four Seasons—Friendship can be seasonal . . .

What, How, When, Where, Who?—This poem was a gift to my 1st wife on our 4th anniversary . . .

Change . . . Evolution . . .—Divorce; due to the subject matter, I didn't feel the title should be included with the actual poem . . .

Seasoned—The 2nd poem written to my 1st wife. It was an attempt of reconciliation . . . however, I wrote it with the ex-girlfriend from **Un-Touchable, Believable, Forgotten?** in mind, as well . . . can you see my smirk?

Friend—I have always had an issue with considering someone to be a "true" friend . . .

Chapter 4—Rome is Burning

Rome is Burning is symbolized by a merging of The Great Fire of Rome (during the rule of Roman emperor Nero) and the decadent, extravagant, and immoral lifestyles of Popes, such as Alexander VI, during Early modern Rome (the latter half of the 15th century). I started many fires in many Romes during this particular time in my life . . .

Narcissistic—Seems a little pompous and self-centered . . . until you get to the end . . .

Delilah, Jezebel, Stella—I was involved with three cougars simultaneously (two of whom were married). The names chosen for this poem not only describe the three women as individuals, but also categorize women in general as I saw them then. The *beauty* of this poem lies within its stanza structure. The 1ˢᵗ line of each stanza refers to Delilah. The 2ⁿᵈ line refers to Jezebel. The 3ʳᵈ line refers to Stella. In essence, there are three poems in one …

Tree House—Be careful of what you do to gain access to someone's heart …

Ladybug—Whenever you see a ladybug, you want to *handle* it with the gentlest touch. This particular *ladybug*, I wanted her to have only **my** touch …

Internal Fire—My entire being was simply on fire for the *ladybug* …

My Dear Lady—My adulterous ways led me to pondering about and writing letters to my ideal woman …

Book II—The Journeyman

After wreaking havoc and causing mass destruction within my own land, I aimlessly traveled into the lands of *others* with a peculiar mentality, quicksilver tongue, and body of reckless abandon as my only weapons at hand …

Chapter 1—The Ring (Removed)

Understanding that the "ring finger" was chosen specifically because it is the only finger that has a blood vessel that runs from the finger, itself, directly to the heart, I tried to respect the symbolic significance of wearing my wedding ring until my divorce was finalized. But, once the marriage was officially dissolved …

First Encounter—During my very first visit to a strip club, I found out the waitress are, sometimes, better than the strippers...

Beautiful—A relationship of a couple of months; the physical solidification of my fascination of *that* particular *woman*...

The Sweetest Sound—Silence can have more impact than the most carefully thought out words. Silence speaks volumes when *ears* are open...

She Does Exist—I've always taken pleasure in using quick wit and sensual spontaneity. I thought I was unrivaled... **and** unmatched... until I met her...

...**The Coexistence**—I was coined Papa Bear by my 1st wife's father. He said I was like an elder in a youth's body. Black Pearl is a moniker given to me by my Freshman English teacher in college. He said my writing style was a special rarity, like a black pearl...

Chapter 2—Uncharted Waters

Uncharted Waters represents a coming of age in being comfortable with certain aspects of my life; brought on by one young lady in particular...

Nature—She was **so** innocently blessed by God. And to compliment her even more, she didn't even know it...

Pumpkin—I take great caution in who I give pet names to and what those pet names are. For her, it came out of nowhere... without warning... without thought...

Undress—I had taken her mind completely out of its clothes, and while trying to give her reason to undress my body, I realized she had already done the same to me…

Nymphony—Symphonies move me. I love the sound of instruments. I love playing instruments… I love the body… the body **is** an instrument…

Why You So Soon—**She** was perfect … time, or the lack thereof, was never an issue…

Man of Steel—**She** actually wrote this poem. In conversation, she paralleled my life in correlation to her perception of my physical being. I simply put it on paper for her. I don't think **anyone** will **ever** be able to do what **she** did during that conversation…

Stalked—Loneliness is **always** around the corner…

When Nothing Else Matters—Nothing else seems to matter when your mind is consumed by the thoughts of *that* special person…

The Gambler—You are sitting at the Blackjack table … and Life is the dealer…

Chips Ahoy—Satan was getting on my nerves … (I was eating chocolate chip cookies when I wrote this poem.)

Just a Taste—With nothing more than a simple kiss, she showed me everything… almost…

Chapter 3—The Elements' Cataclysms

As destructive as life's waters, winds, dirt, rain, sleet, and snow may be, they can **and** will join forces ... earthquakes, floods, tornadoes, hurricanes, blizzards, mudslides, and tsunamis ensue ...

Really?—Be true to yourself in what you do to gain affectionate favor ...

That Word ...—...is love ...

Daylight Savings—Only if the age were younger . . . or older ...

The Cumuli—On cloud nine . . . (This poem was written from the end to the beginning.)

Right (Write) 'On, Nigga! (Why I Write)—Someone questioned me in why I *wasted* my time writing ...

Sunshine—There was a particular young doctor that I saw every day at work. I wasn't particularly attracted to her, but her smile had such a positive effect on me. It was so ... genuine ...

Vitamin B—Her name began with the letter "B" ...

Indoor Rain—The rain of the heart is sometimes light and happy, and at other times, dark and heavy ...

Shut Up—There will **always** be somebody that has suh'em (something) negative to say ...

What Is It? . . . Again!—Sometimes, you just simply get lost in all of the wonderful things about a person . . .

A Daughter's Touch—I have yet to find a feeling more satisfying than the touch of my daughter . . .

Lupercalia—Valentine's Day . . .

Full Bloom—Everything about her was immaculate . . . everything!

Just Wait—While writing another letter to my ideal woman, I was unconsciously coercing myself to wait for her arrival . . .

Now or Later—Patience is a virtue: one that I didn't have, but was trying to gain (Take note of the rhyme scheme.) . . .

Can't Wait—She didn't want to rush. She wanted to wait until I was *officially* available so that her conscious would be clear . . .

Always There—Again, my only unfinished poem . . . unfinished for reasons already discussed. I don't find this poem, or any written reference to it, to be worthy of any visual enhancements . . .

Rock or Hard Place?—When it rains, it pours . . . and a raincoat isn't always helpful . . .

Lucky's Charms—I wrote this poem in parallel to the cereal, Lucky Charms; Lucky just seems to tease whomever whenever and wherever he wants to … with his *charms*, of course …

Chapter 4—The Oasis

After a long and lonely journey to, and through, unfamiliar lands, I wandered upon an oasis of comfort and confidence. Little did I know, it was my next battlefield …

Which Is It?—That which is genuine can have ulterior motives and that which is obviously scheme-ish can have some element of good about it. Either way … you tend to like it …

Breathe—I was trying to breathe a little life into finding that ideal woman …

Euphoric Lovely Excellence—This poem was a birthday gift to someone special. I made reference to her identity in the title itself, and I spelled out her name within the poem …

Slitheran—My perspective of my fellas, Slitheran House … before I entered; from the outside lookin' in …

A. P. B.—I wasn't playin' around with her … this one was *mine* … even though she was already *gone* …

Morning Sickness— … waking up lonely.

Control Burning—Control burning is the process of burning a field of dead grass so that the field may produce a blanket new of grass … I was in the process of regaining control of my spirituality …

Black & White—It is always better to be in the light, but there **are** times of needed darkness...

Peek-A-Boo Street—The title of this poem was inspired by the name of the Winter Games athlete, Picabo Street... however, it actually refers to women (harlots) whom you don't necessarily see *working* and their door always seems to be open only for you... but it is actually open for others, as well...

See Saw—Dedicated to the woman I considered to be my God-mother... my life will forever miss her words of wisdom, demeanor of discernment, and spirit of intuition...

Say Word—I love words! I couldn't resist weaving in Kama Sutra...

Say What?!?!—Talk is cheap... and, sometimes, actions are even *cheaper*...

Long Winter—This breakup felt hit me harder than what my divorce did...

Who's Feeling What?!—A cousin of mine and I were experiencing similar relational problems. After an in-depth discussion, we realized *we* weren't the ones who were *truly* dealing with problems. This poem is the basis of that discussion. Love ya, Sis!

Fuck You—I would rather he had just stayed where he was... **AWAY**...

You, Too!— . . . love had shown me enough of its sarcastic and grim ways of expressing itself . . .

Snake Eyes—I was determined to not give a 6damn about anyone besides myself (with my daughter being an extension of me, of course) . . .

Book III—An Epic Battle

The oasis was no more and my worst enemy was rebelliously standing in the middle of the battlefield, where he had been patiently waiting for me for over two decades . . . that enemy was me . . .

Chapter 1—Hidden Treasure

While good and evil battled against each other, the good re-discovered treasures buried deep within that would aid in gaining total control. I would rather not battle within, but it is inevitable . . . and it will be ongoing . . . and I welcome it, for I have found a treasure worth battling for . . . my soul . . .

Somebody's Somebody—Every last person **has** to be special to somebody, right?

To the Death—Writing, the piano, and the guitar . . . I love them to death . . .

Have You Ever . . .—Truly special . . . **truly**. A home in Puerto Rico would be nice . . .

Half Full Half Empty—Realizing there is **always** room for improvement should not be that difficult . . .

Simple Song . . .—Life will become tougher as we become older. We have to use what we learn to make life bearable . . .

I Forgot To Remember—People always say, "Forget the past." Bananas!!! Don't ever forget your past. Learn from your negatives and improve your positives. Remember your past . . . just don't re-live it. Re-invent your future . . .

Hidden Treasures—I wrote this in remembrance of my eldest uncle . . . be careful of the secrets you hold . . . and the things you keep hidden . . .

Eternal Lifelong Eternity—YES, I did . . . I wrote her **another** birthday poem. This time, throughout the poem, I spelled out a pet-name we had for each other . . . multiple times . . .

Your Hands—In response to the 2nd birthday poem, she inquired about that of her that had the most impactful effect on me emotionally and the seriousness of that effect . . . I loved her physical hands, but she touched me best with her intangible "hands" . . .

Arial—That is what we were going to name her . . .

When the Shoe Fits . . .— . . . it seems so natural just to wear it. I never got too close to circles of friends, but this one was right up my alley . . .

The Day We First Met—The author wrote this poem about the day she and I met . . .

Charm School—Charm and charisma are great attributes to have…and it has become second nature for me to operate through them…

My "Piece"—Though the man I had grown to be was not at all one of perfection, I had found peace in being me…

Fire, Flame, Friction—The Slitheran House Anthem . . . There are unlimited trails to blaze when a wildfire has complete control of itself…

Blurry Vision—Making the trip to pick up my daughter will always be my favorite trip . . . the trip to take her back will always be my worst…

Chapter 2—Re-Masted

After a battle, there is always destruction of some sort. My vessel was beaten, battered, tattered, and bruised, BUT it was still afloat. My mast needed repair desperately, but once done, my sail was ready to catch wind again…the wind known as the breath of God…

The New YOUth—Succeeding generations set the precedence for preceding generations for when the preceding is no longer capable of maintaining…Be mindful of the new *you*. It is not looking pretty…

Change—I wanted to be a breath of fresh air as an educator. It seems neither the students, nor higher ranks of education, were ready for it…

Gone Camping—In avoidance of an extensive removal from society, I entered hibernation instead. Throughout that period of time, there were a bundle of thoughts that consistently crossed my mind … **every day** …

Achy Knees—Regardless of whether your knees ache due to carrying burdens or praying for burdens, God can take away the pain … just talk to him …

Goodbye, and Hello—Regardless of the breakdown of our engagement, I cannot deny the impact she had on my maturation of being a man in an intimate relationship …

Epiphany—I believe God's delight is the delight he gets from his children … He, yet again, had to show me that I was made in His image …

Iscariot—Who is my great enemy and greatest ally? Me … and **only** me …

While Amongst the Lost—While incarcerated, God revealed to me my true purpose for existing … to trail blaze, with my blaze burning for others …

"With controversy comes conviction. With conviction comes awareness. With awareness comes the opportunity for growth."

Derrick E. Sumral

June 23, 2011